*Developmental*
MANAGEMENT

# Greening Business

## MANAGING FOR SUSTAINABLE DEVELOPMENT

JOHN DAVIS

WITH A FOREWORD BY
RONNIE LESSEM

Basil Blackwell

For Ben, James and Kim
and for all the children of the world
whose future depends on 'sustainable development'

Copyright © John Davis 1991, 1994
Foreword © Ronnie Lessem 1991, 1994

First published 1991
First published in paperback 1994

Blackwell Publishers
108 Cowley Road, Oxford, OX4 1JF, UK

238 Main Street
Cambridge, Massachusetts 02142, USA

*British Library Cataloguing in Publication Data*

A CIP catalogue record for this book is available from
the British Library.

*Library of Congress Cataloging in Publication Data*

A CIP catalog record for this book is available from
the Library of Congress.

ISBN 0–631–17202–5
ISBN 0–631–19315–4 (paper)

Typeset in 11 on 13 pt Ehrhardt
by Hope Services (Abingdon) Ltd.
Printed in Great Britain by
T.J. Press Ltd., Padstow, Cornwall.

## Developmental MANAGEMENT

# GREENING BUSINESS

LEARNING SUPPORT SERVICES

City College NORWICH

Please return on or before the
last date stamped below

## Developmental Management
*General Editor*: Ronnie Lessem

Charting the Corporate Mind
*Charles Hampden-Turner**

Managing in the Information Society
*Yoneji Masuda*

Developmental Management
*Ronnie Lessem*

Foundations of Business
*Ivan Alexander*

Greening Business
*John Davis*

Ford on Management
*Henry Ford**

Managing Your Self
*Jagdish Parikh*

Managing the Developing Organization
*Bernard Lievegoed*

Conceptual Toolmaking
*Jerry Rhodes*

Integrative Management
*Pauline Graham*

Total Quality Learning
*Ronnie Lessem*

Executive Leadership
*Elliott Jaques and Stephen D. Clement*

Transcultural Management
*Albert Koopman*

The Great European Illusion
*Alain Minc*

The Rise of NEC
*Koji Kobayashi*

Organizing Genius
*Paul Thorne*

European Strategic Alliances
*Sabine Urban and Serge Vendemini*

\* For copyright reasons this edition is not available in the USA

The inhabitants of planet earth are quietly conducting a gigantic environmental experiment. So vast and so sweeping will be the impacts of this experiment that, were it brought before any responsible council for approval, it would be firmly rejected as having potentially dangerous consequences. The experiment in question is the release of carbon dioxide and other so-called 'greenhouse gases' to the atmosphere.

Wallace S. Broecker; evidence to a US Senate Committee

The onus of proving that sustainable development is feasible rests primarily on the private business sector, as it controls most of the technological and productive capacity needed to conceive more environmentally benign processes, products and services, and to introduce them throughout the world.

We can and must mobilise this capacity. We should seize the business opportunities offered by green consumerism, recycling, waste minimisation and energy efficiency, and at the same time show corporate responsibility and commitment of a high order in reducing the strain on the environment and in developing innovative solutions.

Peter Wallenberg; President of the International Chamber of Commerce

# Acknowledgements

The author and publisher wish to thank the following who have kindly given permission for the use of copyright material: June Hall Literary Agency and Collins Publishers, London for allowing us to quote from John Harvey-Jones's *Making it Happen*; Celltech Limited for figure 10.2; Unilever for figure 10.1; The Director of the International Chamber of Commerce UK for the quotation from Peter Wallenberg; Mrs Schumacher for quotations from E. F. Schumacher; Mercury Books for a quotation from Sir John Egan. Every effort has been made to trace all copyright holders, but if any have been inadvertently overlooked, the publishers will be pleased to make the necessary arrangement at the first opportunity.

# Contents

# Guest Foreword

The scale, the courage, the demanding vision in this book makes it an exceptional read for any manager. There are all the signs of the future in this book. The future is a bouquet of nettles – business and society will have to reach out of its rut and grasp them.

The future we are patterning for ourselves pays no regard to the limits of the earth. Mr Davis, with an unusual blend of authority, experience and openness of mind and heart, brings into focus the urgency with which we in business must address our growing social responsibilities. He raises the formidable realities of environmental policy for industry, but more than that he relates it to the key issues of company law, of democracy at work, of the inevitable changes that we must impose upon ourselves. This is a brave work.

I commend this work for its breadth, foresightedness and its meticulous and practical relevance to our human predicament. It shows there is more, much more, to management than e'er we thought in our professional philosophy.

Sir Peter Parker

# Foreword: Greening Management

## BY RONNIE LESSEM

## Introduction

In the late eighties it seems the 'greens' came of age. In the past decade, all over Western Europe, they made tremendous strides at the polls, and the likelihood is that they will begin to assert themselves in Eastern Europe in the coming decade. Environmental issues, however, are global and the Brazilians, the Indonesians, the Americans and the Japanese, in fact the United Nations as a whole, have recently become seriously concerned with the problems of the ozone layer. No other issue has produced such a strong awareness of our global interdependence.

The response of the international business community to this new, global imperative has been purposeful, cautious and pragmatic. There has been no one to guide their efforts, or at least so it has seemed. No guiding philosophy seems to have emerged to which they might adhere.

### Small is Beautiful

In fact this is not the case. For in the early seventies a German economist, E. F. Schumacher, who spent most of his working life in Britain, became a champion of what he called 'economics as if people mattered'. Having taught economics at Columbia University in New York from the age of 22, Schumacher published his book *Small is Beautiful* in 1973.[1] It had an immediate impact on the world, not as an economic or ecological treatise, but through its influence on entrepreneurship.

In fact the resurgence of small business, in both developed and developing nations, owes more to Fritz Schumacher than to the free market economists and politicians of the day. Yet Schumacher himself was hardly a free marketeer!

The trouble was that in the mid-seventies the business world was only half ready for Schumacher. In Britain, for example, his disciple John Davis began to establish what became known as 'local enterprise trusts'. These trusts, based on Schumacher's ideas, were the forerunners of the Enterprise Agencies now spread throughout the country, which, as public–private partnerships, have been stimulating locally based, new and small enterprises for more than a decade. Schumacher's other disciple, George Macrobie, spearheaded the formation and development of the 'Intermediate Technology Group', which has been stimulating the growth of small-scale or 'appropriate' technology throughout the developing world.

## Sustainable Development

John Davis started out in life not as an economic or ecological evangelist but as an engineer. In his youth he explored the frontiers of technology with Rolls Royce before beginning his managerial career at Shell. After rising to positions of successively greater responsibility, he ultimately became chairman and managing director of one of the multinational's subsidiaries. It was then that he first met Schumacher.

In mid-life Davis underwent a major transition, from executive to enabler, from organization man to community developer. Having adopted the causes of both small business and intermediate technology, he became a champion of local economic development in Great Britain. For Davis, as for Schumacher, small was beautiful. Having spent most of his working life in one of the world's largest companies, Davis in his fifties entered his age of renewal, reaching into that entrepreneurial and developmental part of himself that had lain half dormant for so many years. More recently, in maturity, Davis has taken the further step of integrating the two parts of himself, the manager and the enabler, to become champion of both small- and large-scale business. In order to realize himself, in this integrated way, he has had to espouse the whole of Schumacher's philosophy rather than just a part of it. In so doing he has become an economist and an ecologist, an engineer and an entrepreneur. What then has been the overall philosophy that has inspired Davis to stretch himself in this way, to evolve his own theory and practice of sustainable development for managers?

# The Whole of Management

## The Attraction of Opposites

Schumacher's unique contribution to developmental management lies not in his adoption of the entrepreneurial cause, but in his linking western and eastern philosophies with business and economic principles. Such philosophies combined his European and Christian heritage with his devotion to nature and his reverence for Buddhism.

For Schumacher, moreover, the true challenges of living – in politics, economics, education or family relationships – inevitably lay in reconciling opposites. Such problem-solving demanded not only the employment of reasoning powers but the commitment of the whole personality. Hence superficial solutions never endure because they invariably neglect one of the two opposites and so lose the full quality of life.

In industry, for example, efficiency measures might provide for discipline but not for participation, and might therefore fail to enhance productivity in the long run. As a result, in Hampden Turner's terms,[2] management will fail to resolve a dilemma. Schumacher, in effect, was particularly concerned with seven kinds of dilemma that directly impinged upon business and economic performance. While John Davis has alluded to each of these, indirectly, in building up his managerial path to sustainable development, I shall take the opportunity in this introduction to refer to them directly. For they provide some of the most fertile grounds for developmental management in general.

## Capitalism and Socialism

At a time of great change in Eastern Europe it is instructive to read what Schumacher has to say about these two great 'isms'. There is no simple solution, he says, either capitalistic or socialistic, to the problem of economic development. Whereas the former, if exclusively followed, leads to the destruction of the dignity of man, the latter leads to a chaotic kind of efficiency – witness the Soviet Union in the early nineties.

Denying both these solutions in isolation, Schumacher calls for a 'living solution' achieved day by day on a basis of clear recognition that both opposites have validity.

In fact Schumacher is horrified by the attempt to oversimplify reality, made by both capitalists and socialists. While raw capitalism reduces a living quality (the product) to lifeless quantity (monetary profit), raw socialism reduces Marx's workers of the world to a Stalinist dictatorship. What Schumacher proposes instead, as exemplified by the well-known British cooperative enterprise, Scott Bader, is the recognition of four equally important business tasks:

- The *economic* task, to secure orders which can be designed, made and serviced in such a manner as to make a profit;
- the *technical* task, to enable marketing to secure profitable orders by keeping them supplied with up-to-date product design;
- the *social* task, to provide members of the company with opportunities for satisfaction and development through participation in the working community;
- the *political* task, to encourage other men and women to change society by offering them an example of economic health and social responsibility.

For Schumacher, at both a micro and macro level there needs to be a balance between a managed economic and technical order, and free social and political expression.

## Freedom and Order

In my book on developmental management,[3] I have argued that Europe's essential contribution to the world is to resolve the dichotomy between freedom and order, in business as well as in social and political life. In the final analysis, Schumacher argues, the question of size of business unit is not one to be answered by managerial economists but by political philosophers.

In the affairs of men, there always appears to be a need for at least two things simultaneously, which, on the face of it, seem to be incompatible and to exclude one another. We always need both freedom and order. We need the freedom of lots and lots of small, autonomous units, and, at the same time, the orderliness of large-scale, possibly global, unity and co-ordination.[4]

For when it comes to action, he says, we obviously need small units, because action is a highly personal affair, and one cannot be in touch with more than a very limited number of people at any one time. However, when it comes to the world of ideas, to principles or to ethics, to the indivisibility of peace and of ecology, we need to recognize the unity of mankind and base our actions upon this recognition.

Interestingly enough, Schumacher's claim that 'small is beautiful' was born out of a metaphysical and social approach to economics rather than out of a physical and monetary one. In fact the subtitle of his book introduces economics as if people mattered!

What is the meaning of democracy, freedom, human dignity, standard of living, self-realisation, fulfilment? Is it a matter of goods, or of people? Of course it is a matter of people. But people can be themselves only in small comprehensible groups. Therefore we must learn to think in terms of an articulated structure that can cope with a multiplicity of small-scale units. If economic thinking cannot grasp this it is useless. If it cannot get beyond its vast abstractions, the national income, the rate of growth, . . . and make contact with the human realities of poverty, frustration, . . . congestion, ugliness and spiritual death, then let us scrap economics and start afresh.[5]

Schumacher, as an academic and applied economist, certainly did start afresh, qualitatively rather than quantitatively. He formulated five principles of organization which were to become his hallmark as an economist among such members of the business community as John Davis, even if not in the economic establishment, whether fiscal or monetarist.

1   *The principle of subsidiarity*   In the first instance, for Schumacher, it is an injustice and even a grave evil to assign to a greater and higher association what lesser and subordinate organizations can do.

The structure of the organization may then be symbolized by someone holding a large number of balloons. Each of the balloons has its own buoyancy and lift. Each balloon becomes an administrative as well as an entrepreneurial unit. What role is to be played by the person holding the balloons? This brings us to Schumacher's second principle of 'vindication'.

2   *The principle of vindication*   Good government, or good management, according to Schumacher, is always by exception. In other words, apart from exceptional cases, the subsidiary unit must be defended against reproach, upheld and vindicated. While profit must be the final criterion of the unit's success, it is not always possible to apply it mechanically. If it enjoys special and inescapable advantages it must pay a rent, and if it has to cope with inescapable disadvantages it must be granted a special subsidy.

3  *The principle of identification*   Each subsidiary unit must have, according to the principle of identification, a profit and loss account and balance sheet. The balance sheet describes the economic substance as augmented or diminished by current results. Profits and losses are carried forward and not wiped out. Therefore it is of great psychological importance to the subsidiary unit, whether it be Scotland in the context of the UK or Acorn Computers in the context of Olivetti, that profits can appear as loans to the centre and losses as loans from the centre.

4  *The principle of motivation*   For a large organization, with its bureaucracies, its remote and impersonal controls, its many abstract rules and regulations and, above all, the relative incomprehensibility that stems from its size, motivation is a central problem. At the top level this is no problem, but lower down the problem becomes increasingly acute. Japan has succeeded economically because large-scale organizations have managed to harness the motivation of all their people by, amongst other things, the cellular structure of their economic units.

5  *The principle of the middle axiom*   Finally Schumacher returns to his starting point. All human and organizational problems stem from the tension between order and freedom. Without order, planning, predictability, central control, accountancy, instructions to subordinates, obedience and discipline, nothing can happen, because everything disintegrates. And yet, without the magnanimity of disorder, a certain happy abandon and the willingness of the creative imagination to approach the unknown and incalculable, life is a mockery and a disgrace. How painfully aware Michail Gorbachev must have been of this particular dichotomy after taking over from Brezniev.

For while the centre can look after order it is much more difficult to oversee freedom and creativity, whether in a division of General Motors or in the USSR's Baltic states. This is where Schumacher's principle of the middle axiom helps. Neither the gentle method of government by exhortation nor the tough method of government by instruction meets the requirements in either case. What is required is something in between, a middle axiom, an order from above which is not quite an order.

Discovering such a middle axiom is always a considerable achievement. For Mao Tse-Tung at the height of his power it involved going to the practical people and learning from them, synthesizing their practices into principles and theories, then calling upon them to put these principles into practice, in order to solve their problems and achieve freedom and happiness.


## Man and Nature

### *The Limits of the Market*

Economics, for Schumacher, has not only to concern itself with the resolution of the dichotomy between freedom and man-made order but also with achieving a balance between free enterprise and the natural order. What preoccupies Schumacher is that mainstream economics, whether capitalist or socialist, ignored man's dependence on the natural world. The market therefore represents only the surface of society and its

significance relates to the momentary situation as it exists there and then. There is no probing into the depths of things, into the natural or social facts that lie behind them. In a sense, the market is the institutionalisation of individualism and non-responsibility. . . . To equate things means to give them a price and thus to make them exchangeable. To the extent that economic thinking is based on the market, it takes the sacredness out of life, because there can be nothing sacred in something that has a price.[6]

Every science, Schumacher argues, is beneficial within its proper limits, but becomes evil and destructive as soon as it transgresses them. Economic science, if it is to retain its proper place, has to remain subservient to what might be called 'meta-economics'. Such a meta-discipline deals first with the individual human being and secondly with his or her environment. In other words we may expect that economics must derive its aims and objectives from the study of man, and that it must derive a large part of its methodology from a study of nature.


### *The Function of Work*

To help in the development of such a meta-discipline the western Christian, Schumacher, always seeking to reconcile opposites, turns to eastern Buddhism for inspiration. There is universal agreement, he says, that a fundamental source of human wealth is labour. Certainly Henry Ford subscribed to this belief.[7] However, whereas the orthodox economist considers labour to be a mere factor of production, the Buddhist takes the function of work to be at least threefold:

- to give man a chance to develop and utilize his faculties;
- to enable him to overcome his egocentricity by joining with other people in a common task;
- to bring forth the goods and services needed for a becoming existence.

It is no accident, of course, that this attitude to work is more prevalent in Buddhist Japan than it is in Christian Europe and America.

The Buddhist, moreover, at least according to Schumacher, sees the essence of civilization not in a multiplication of wants but in the purification of human character. Here we may begin to part company, to some extent, with modern Japan. Character, however, is primarily formed by a person's work. An Indian philosopher, Kumarappa, sums up the matter as follows:

If the nature of work is properly appreciated and applied, it will stand in the same relation to the higher faculties as food is to the physical body. It nourishes and enlivens the higher man and urges him to produce the best he is capable of. It directs his free will along the proper course and disciplines the animal in him into progressive channels. It furnishes an excellent background for man to display his scale of values and develop his personality.[8]

It is not surprising, therefore, that Jagdish Parikh, who has written for the Developmental Management series,[9] is an Indian. In his book he argues that effective work should become a means towards self-development rather than vice versa.

*Living with Nature*

So much for the nature of man. What lessons, for management and for economics, does Schumacher draw from nature itself? He says that the fundamental principle of agriculture, as opposed to industry, is that it deals with living substances. Its products are the results of processes of life and its means of production is the living soil.

The management of the land (as a living substance, a cubic centimetre of fertile soil contains millions of living organisms) must be primarily oriented towards three goals – health, beauty and permanence. A fourth goal, productivity, will then be attained almost as a by-product. This is a theme upon which I have elaborated in relation not specifically to agriculture but to business as a whole.[10]

Whereas the narrowly based economic perspective limits agriculture to food production, a wider and wiser point of view involves agriculture in:

- keeping the individual in touch with living nature, of which he or she remains a highly vulnerable part;
- humanizing and enobling man's wider habitat;
- bringing forth the foodstuffs and other materials that are needed for a becoming life.

## *The Economics of Permanence*

For Schumacher the cultivation and expansion of needs is the antithesis of wisdom. Every increase of needs tends to increase one's dependence on outside forces. Gandhi said that 'the earth provides enough for every man's need but not for every man's greed.' Permanence is incompatible with a predatory attitude. A person driven by greed or envy, Schumacher emphasizes, loses the power of seeing things as they really are, of seeing things in their wholeness. Cleverness abounds but there is no wisdom. After a while even the Gross National Product refuses to rise any further, not because of scientific or technological failure, but because of a creeping paralysis of non-cooperation. 'Instead of overcoming the "world" by moving towards saintliness, [man] tries to overcome it by gaining pre-eminence'.[11] This brings us to what Schumacher describes as our greatest resource – education.

## Matter and Spirit

Although Schumacher did not live long enough to see the full flowering of the information age, he anticipated the growth and development of the knowledge-based economy. He foresaw that it was 'the mind of man', not land, not capital, that provided the key factor in economic development. Anticipating, in a remarkable way, the current education debate, in which Great Britain and the United States are unfavourably compared with Japan and South Korea, he maintained that 'if Western civilisation is in a state of permanent crisis, it is not far fetched to suggest that there may be something wrong with its education.'

However, Schumacher has a particular view on education, which contrasts with today's conventional wisdom. For him know-how, so highly valued by the current business and political establishment in the democratic world, is a means without an end, a mere potentiality, an unfinished sentence, a piano without music. The essence of education is the transmission of values, not as mere assertions or formulae, but as instruments through which we look at, interpret and experience the world. Education cannot help us, Schumacher says, as long as it ignores metaphysics, that is the source of our fundamental convictions. Economics, for example, can only be considered part of our genuine education if it is taught with an awareness of the view of human nature that underlies it.

All subjects, no matter how specialised, are connected with a centre; they are like rays emanating from a sun. The centre is constituted by our most basic convictions, by those ideas which really have the power to move us. . . . Education can help us only if it produces 'whole men'. . . . the conduct of his life will show a certain sureness of touch which stems from his inner clarity.[12]

Such centres are the places where individuals have to create orderly systems of ideas about who they are, which can regulate the direction of their various strivings. In the final analysis, then, education which fails to clarify our central convictions, as individuals or as a whole society, is mere training or indulgence.

## Wealth and Poverty

### Economic Development

Schumacher's views of education are naturally closely aligned with his developmental philosophy. The primary causes of poverty, as far as he is concerned, are immaterial, lying in certain deficiencies in education, organization and discipline. Without these three all resources remain latent, untapped potential. Development does not start with goods: it starts with people and their education. Those countries after the last war, notably West Germany and Japan, that had a high level of education, organization and discipline, produced economic miracles. 'In fact, these were miracles only for people whose attention is focused on the tip of the iceberg. The tip had been smashed to pieces, but the base, which is education, organisation, and discipline, was still there'.[13]

Here lies the central problem of development, whether for individuals or for organizations, for economic regions or for whole cultures. Here lies the reason why development cannot be an act of creation, why it cannot be ordered, bought or comprehensively planned, why it requires a process of evolution. Education does not jump; it is a gradual process of great subtlety. Organization does not jump; it must gradually evolve to fit changing circumstances. Much the same goes for discipline. All three must evolve step by step, and the foremost task of development must be to speed this evolution. All three must, moreover, become the property not merely of a tiny minority but of the society as a whole.

If capital or aid is given to introduce new business or economic activities these will be beneficial and viable only if they can be sustained by the already existing educational level of fairly broad groups of people. They will be truly valuable only if they promote and spread advances in education, organization and discipline. This applies equally to the Indian national railways, to the Greek banking system, to the economy of Zimbabwe.

There can be a process of stretching, Schumacher maintains, but never a process of jumping. If new business or economic activities are introduced which depend on special education, special discipline and special organization such as are in no way inherent in the recipient organization or society, the activity will not promote healthy development but will hinder it. Like a misplaced acquisition it will remain a foreign body that cannot be integrated and will exacerbate the problems of the developing business or society.

## Technology Development

Schumacher's views on what he called intermediate or appropriate technology follow directly from his views on economic development. Having observed, around the globe, that in the seventies the poor were getting poorer and the rich richer, he calls into fundamental question the conventional wisdom on economic aid and technology transfer. For Schumacher it is more important that everybody should produce something than that a few should produce a great deal. In that respect he follows in Gandhi's footsteps.

The real task, he says, may be formulated in four propositions:

- first, that workplaces have to be created in the areas where the people are living now, and not primarily in metropolitan areas in which they tend to migrate;

- second, that these workplaces must be, on average, built cheaply enough to be created in large numbers without this calling for an unattainable level of capital formation and imports;
- third, that the production methods employed must be relatively simple, so that the demands for high skills are minimized, not only in the production process itself but also in matters of organization, raw material supply, finance and marketing;
- fourth, that production should be mainly from local materials and mainly for local use.

It is this approach to technology development that inspired John Davis to establish local enterprise trusts not in Belize or in Bangladesh but in the United Kingdom. True to Schumacher's orientation towards the reconciliation of opposites we find ourselves, today, living in a world where an accelerating trend towards global interdependence is matched by an increasing demand for local independence, both political and economic.


## Technology and Society

The primary concern of technology, for Schumacher, is to lighten the burden of work that man has to carry in order to stay alive and develop his potential. In that respect Schumacher and Ford, seemingly unlikely bedfellows, would be in total agreement. Can we ensure that we develop such a technology, Schumacher asks, that really helps us solve our problems, that is a technology with a human face.

Technology recognizes no self-limiting principle in terms of, for instance, size, speed or violence. It therefore does not possess the virtues of being self-balancing, self-adjusting and self-cleansing. In the subtle system of nature, technology acts as a foreign body, and there are now numerous signs of rejection, global warming being the most frightening of all.

Suddenly, if not altogether surprisingly, the modern world, shaped by modern technology, finds itself involved in three crises simultaneously. First, human nature revolts against inhuman technological, organisational, and political patterns, which it experiences as suffocating and debilitating; second, the living environment which supports human life aches and groans and gives signs of partial breakdown; and, third, it is clear to anyone fully knowledgeable in the subject matter that the inroads being made into the world's non-renewable resources, particularly those of fossil fuels, are such that serious bottlenecks and virtual exhaustion loom ahead in the quite foreseeable future.[14]

Although, over the course of the past twenty years, emphasis has shifted from an impending scarcity of fossil fuels to a preoccupation with the world's rainforests, Schumacher was undoubtedly pointing in the right general direction. What is clear for him, as for his disciple Davis, is that a way of life based on limitless material expansion in a finite environment cannot last long. Technology has to be redirected so that it serves man rather than destroys him. In fact Schumacher perceptively pointed out, some twenty years ago, that the content of politics is economics, and the main content of economics is technology. If politics cannot be left to the experts, he argues, nor can economics or technology.

## Capital and Income

The root problem, as far as Schumacher is concerned, lies in western man's attitude to nature and, since the whole world is in a process of westernization, the problem has become a global one. For the modern people do not experience themselves as part of nature but as outside forces destined to dominate and conquer it.

The illusion of unlimited powers, nourished by astonishing scientific and technological achievements, has produced the concurrent illusion of having solved the problem of production. The latter illusion is based on the failure to distinguish between income and capital where this distinction matters most. . . . namely, the irreplaceable capital which man has not made, but simply found, and without which he can do nothing.[15]

A businessman would not consider a firm to have solved its problems of production and to have achieved viability if he saw that it was rapidly consuming its capital. How, then, could we overlook this vital factor when we consider that very big firm, the economy of Spaceship Earth and, in particular, the economies of its rich passengers? To use the language of the economist, they live on irreplaceable capital which they cheerfully treat as income.

# Conclusion

## The Universal Message

There has never been a time, Schumacher concludes, in any society in any part of the world, without its sages and teachers to challenge materialism and plead for a different order of priorities. The languages have differed, the symbols have varied, yet the message has always been the same: 'seek ye first the kingdom of God, and these things [the material things which you also need] shall be added unto you'. The developmental approach to management implies that the holistic principles of business must come first; the rational and primal ones follow.

Today, however, this message reaches us not only from the sages and saints but also from the course of physical events. It speaks to us in the language of terrorism, genocide, breakdown, pollution, and exhaustion. We live, it seems, in a unique period of convergence. It is becoming apparent that there is not only a promise but also a threat, that unless you seek first the kingdom, these other things which you need will cease to be available to you.

Out of the whole Christian tradition, Schumacher claims, there is no body of teaching that is more relevant and appropriate to the modern predicament than 'the four cardinal virtues'.

## The Four Cardinal Virtues

The meaning of *prudentia*, significantly called the mother of all virtues, is not conveyed by the modern word prudence. It signifies, in fact, the opposite of a small, mean, calculating attitude to life.

The pre-eminence of prudence means that realisation of the good presupposes knowledge of reality. He alone can do good who knows what things are like and what their situation is. The pre-eminence of prudence means that so called good intentions, and meaning well, by no means suffice. Realisation of the good presupposes that our actions are appropriate to the real situation.[16]

This clear-eyed objectivity, however, cannot be achieved and prudence cannot be perfected except by an attitude of silent contemplation, such as that achieved during meditation,[17] during which the egocentric interests of man are temporarily silenced. Only on the basis of this magnanimous kind of prudence can we achieve the other three cardinal virtues – *justitia*, *fortitudo* and *temperantia*. Justice relates to truth, fortitude to goodness, and temperance to beauty, while prudence – in a sense – comprises all three.

## Inside Out

At the time of my writing this foreword, there is regularly shown on British television a popular commercial depicting the Prudential Insurance Company. It portrays a foreigner in search of the Prudential, who is urged to locate it at 'the Holborn', the road in which it is physically based. As the company is a client of mine, I happen to know that this reflection of the company's outer being is not matched by the kind of inner awareness, of *prudentia*, to which Schumacher alludes. This is hardly surprising, despite the fact that this largest of Britain's insurance companies is going through a phase of vigorous renewal. Having reacquainted myself with Schumacher's philosophy I now have the courage to invite my friends at the Prudential to heed his advice.

Everywhere people ask: 'What can I actually *do*?' The answer is as simple as it is disconcerting: we can, each of us, work to put our own inner house in order. The guidance we need for this work cannot be found in science or technology, the value of which utterly depends on the ends they serve; but it can still be found in the traditional wisdom of mankind.[18]

While the late Fritz Schumacher was an economic philosopher who turned his mind to commercial matters, John Davis is a business executive who turned his mind to philosophical matters. Along the way they met and formed a powerful combination, turning a global idea, 'small is beautiful', into a local reality – the three hundred or so enterprise agencies that have been established in the UK over the past ten years.

Prudence implies a transformation of the knowledge of truth into decisions corresponding to reality. What, therefore, could be of greater importance today than the study and cultivation of the classical notion of prudence? This would inevitably lead to a real understanding of the three other cardinal virtues, all of which are indispensable for the survival of civilization, and would form the basis of sustainable development, through the greening of management. This is the subject of Davis's book.

Ronnie Lessem
London, 1990

## Notes

1  The 1973 edition was published by Blond & Briggs, but my notes refer to the later edition: E. F. Schumacher, *Small is Beautiful: a Study of Economics as if People Mattered*. Abacus, London, 1974.

2  C. Hampden Turner, *Charting the Corporate Mind*. Basil Blackwell, Oxford, 1990.

3  R. Lessem, *Developmental Management*. Basil Blackwell, Oxford, 1990.

4  Schumacher, *Small is Beautiful*, pp. 53–4.

5  Ibid., p. 62.

6  Ibid., pp. 36–7.

7  H. Ford, *Ford on Management*. Basil Blackwell, Oxford, 1990.

8  J. Kumarappa, *Economy of Permanence*. Sarva, 1958.

9  J. Parikh, *Managing the Self*. Basil Blackwell, Oxford, 1990.

10  R. Lessem, *Total Learning – Quality Management*. Basil Blackwell, Oxford, 1990.

11  Schumacher, *Small is Beautiful*, p. 31.

12  Ibid., p. 77.

13  Ibid., p. 140.

14  Ibid., pp. 122–3.

15  Ibid., p. 11.

16  J. Piper, *Justice*. Faber and Faber, London, 1957.

17  Parikh, *Managing the Self*, p. 00.

18  Schumacher, *Small is Beautiful*, pp. 249–50.

# Preface

Early in 1976 the late Dr E. F. Schumacher and I were invited by John Marsh, who was then Director of the British Institute of Management, to a dinner along with a dozen major-company senior executives. I had recently joined him and some of his colleagues to promote action for sustainable development in Britain. The topic for the evening was a discussion of the application to business of the ideas in his book *Small is Beautiful*, the central message of which is that a different kind of economic development, one that is sustainable, has become a globally urgent necessity. After the dinner I was forced to conclude that the companies these executives represented were not yet ready to contemplate changes based on a set of assumptions and beliefs that were at variance with the conventional wisdom of that time.

In 1990 the situation is entirely different. There is now world-wide recognition that a shift to a sustainable form of development is an urgent imperative. Businesses will be the main agent for bringing about change in the direction of development, and consequently a very heavy burden of responsibility falls on all business managers.

It is the magnitude and urgency of the necessary change that are the main justifications for a book on the subject for managers. The threat of the greenhouse effect is imminent. Atmospheric levels of greenhouse gases have to be stabilized at no more than present levels within the next three decades. This requirement is the pace-setter for sustainable development. Obviously, there is no time to lose. The range and scale of the changes required to halt further environmental and ecological damage, while still permitting necessary economic development to proceed globally, cannot be expressed so simply. In Europe, consumption of fossil energy and non-renewable materials needs to be reduced by about two-thirds over the next half century.

Very detailed studies have shown that it is technically feasible; but the target can only be achieved through a fundamental shift in business values from a money driven/consumption to a people centred/ conserver approach. 'Business as usual', with some concessions to limit pollution, would fall far short of what is needed but, against the existing threats, falling short is not something that can be contemplated. Sustainable development demands comprehensive changes in all aspects of business life. The transformation task that faces managements and workforces in all kinds of business is unique because it demands *fundamental* changes in many traditional assumptions and beliefs. There is now no escape from the challenge.

This book is an attempt to assist managers and workpeople of all kinds to grapple with the problems that sustainable development presents. The views expressed have grown out of my own experience as an engineer and a manager at all levels, combined with lessons learned from many friends and colleagues over nearly fifty years. Although I take full responsibility for all the views contained in the book, I want to express my gratitude to all who have helped me to form them, and most of all to Fritz Schumacher himself, who did so much for me in bringing order out of mental chaos.

There are others to whom I wish to give special thanks for the help and advice they have offered in the production of this book. They are George Goyder CBE, Philip Baxendale, Tom McLeod and Ronnie Lessem, the series editor. I also thank my daughter Joanna, who interrupted more congenial activities to produce the typescript, and my wife Jean, who not only undertook the thankless task of proof reading but also patiently tolerated several months in which sustainable development caused me to be mentally abstracted and neglectful.

John Davis
1990

# What does Sustainable Development Mean?

The reality of change is inescapable. If we do not change, the inexorable forces and shifts in the external world will force change upon us. Better to change before we are changed.

John Harvey-Jones*

We are living in very exciting times. They are times of radical change and uncertainty all over the world. A feeling that the ground under our feet is not quite as firm as it used to be adds to our sense of excitement: just how firm it feels depends upon how secure are our basic assumptions and beliefs about life in general, and about business life in particular.

## A Continuity of Change

Life is never static. In the market economies in particular, until quite recently, change has been slow and steady, with no alterations in basic assumptions and beliefs about economic life. Under these conditions administration has played a dominant part in management. Innovation was never the main preoccupation until recently. It was needed from time to time to bring about changes when they became essential, but in most mainstream businesses it was seldom out in front creating change for the sake of change. In general, administration ruled and innovation followed.

Over a long period businesses have been the motive power of economic growth. There has been a gradual development that has had several important characteristics:

1 transfer of work from home to factory, office and shop; and from rural areas to towns;
2 substitution of manufacturing for repair and reconditioning services, leading to a 'throw-away' society;
3 substitution of financial investment for labour through advancing technologies;
4 transformation from a producer-led to a market-led form of business, with the concept of fashion marketing;
5 concentration of activities in a small number of very big industrial and commercial companies, and a decline of small- and medium-sized, locally owned firms;
6 the internationalization of finance and corporate ownership.

All of these characteristics of change have evolved under the influence of an underlying set of assumptions and beliefs about world resources and the environment, about people as consumers, earners and investors, and about the ways in which human skills, energy and ingenuity can best be combined with financial investment for the generation of monetary wealth. Of course, there has not been universal agreement about these assumptions and beliefs: there have been dissident voices throughout the period. However, it is only during the past twenty years that some have begun to take them seriously.


## Environmental Concerns Emerge

The early 1970s saw the publication of *Limits to Growth – a Report of the Club of Rome*, the Report of the 1972 Stockholm Conference of the United Nations on 'The Human Environment' and the late Dr E. F. Schumacher's book *Small is Beautiful*.[1] These can now be seen as seminal events that triggered a debate leading, in the late 1980s, to a global agreement – ranging from the supermarket shopper in the High Street to the General Assembly of the United Nations. It is now believed that if there is a continuation of the kind of development so far known and enjoyed by a quarter of the world's population, it is very likely to lead to such widespread environmental and ecological damage as to amount to the destruction of a large part of the earth's life support system. Thus it is said that the traditional form of economic development, based on a particular set of assumptions and beliefs having the six characteristics listed above, is unsustainable.

Not since the dawn of civilisation some 8,000 years ago has the earth been about 1°C warmer than today. To find conditions like those projected for the middle of the next century, we must go back millions of years. If current trends in 'greenhouse gas' build up continue, we will have committed earth to a warming of 1.5° to 4.5°C by around 2030, the upper end of this range being the more probable. In short, if the 'greenhouse-effect' turns out to be as great as predicted by today's climate models, and if current emission trends continue, our world will soon differ radically from anything in human experience.

*The President, World Resources Institute*[2]

## *A Bleak Prospect for the Year AD 2000*

1 Per capita consumption of food in South East Asia, the Middle East and much of Africa will not improve, and in some places it will decline from its present inadequate level, despite an increase of 90 per cent in global food production.
2 A 25 per cent shortfall in the supply of firewood will have a devastating effect on the quarter of the human race that depends entirely on the use of wood for fuel.
3 40 per cent of the remaining forests will have been destroyed, with the result that many countries will have increasingly erratic supplies of water.
4 An area the size of the state of Maine is becoming barren wasteland each year, and a fifth of all plant and animal species could be lost.

*Source*: The *Global 2000 Report*[3]

Many more study reports, conferences and books have followed culminating in the 1988 Brundtland Report. The most important recommendation is that 'the principle of sustainable development must be built into all activities.'[4]

## Sustainable Development – Changing Assumptions and Beliefs

An understanding of the complex idea of sustainable development can best be approached by contrasting some of the underlying assumptions and beliefs of conventional economic development that affect sustainability. As Schumacher repeatedly pointed out, and as practical consequences demonstrate, each of the six below is flawed.

1 Increasing indiscriminate growth of financial transactions will produce benefits and prosperity for all. (In fact we can see that it widens the gap between rich and poor, and a progressively smaller proportion of the world's population are enjoying the fruits because the 'trickle-down' theory does not work.)
2 Natural resources are believed to be unlimited, and they can be exploited unconditionally; the environment is also unlimited in its capacity to withstand human activity in all its forms. (The consequence is that important non-renewable resources are being rapidly exhausted, and the environment is being destabilized by the activities of only a quarter of the world population.)
3 Capital-intensive manufacturing is universally more efficient and productive than labour-intensive repair and reconditioning services. (In fact the capital-intensive manufacturing system that has been produced is immensely wasteful and environmentally damaging. It has been sustained by some fundamental fallacies in the ways the productivity and efficiency have been measured.)
4 Earning a living is inevitably a demanding activity. All that is needed to satisfy workers is an adequate financial reward; the nature of the work required is of no great importance. (The consequence has been a total failure to optimize the human contribution to wealth creation in the mix of men, money and machines. Human creative effort has far more to offer, if properly organized and employed, both to the economy and to personal satisfaction.)
5 People have an unlimited hunger for possessions. So long as they conform to fashion they are an acceptable mark of social status and the principal means of personal satisfaction. (In fact, as the late Fred Hirsch pointed out,[5] the value placed by individuals on particular desires declines the more widely they are shared by other people. When desires become frustrated they lose their attraction, and life becomes a series of frustrations. Once material needs have been satisfied, self-fulfilment has to be gained in non-material ways.)
6 So long as growth and/or a good return can be obtained on savings, people are in general not concerned who invests them nor what

purpose they are intended to serve. (The consequence has been that personal financial power has been given away to impersonal financial institutions; they use it for their own purposes, which often do not correspond with the real interests of the individual or the general community good. Ethical investment schemes indicate that a growing number of people are not happy to leave investment choice entirely in the hands of others.)

If these are the underlying assumptions and beliefs that underpin an unsustainable kind of development, what are the concepts which can be used to replace them in order to promote a sustainable economic development?

**Box 1** *Some Assumptions and Beliefs for Sustainable Development*

(a) Of Economies

- Economic activity should not only be efficient in its use of all resources but should also be socially just, and environmentally and ecologically sustainable.
- The purpose should be to satisfy all human needs – physical, mental, emotional and spiritual – through personal responsibility, mutual aid and governmental enabling, with minimum consumption of scarce resources.
- Communities need to develop economic self-reliance as a basis for dignity and self-determination.
- Inter-trading should primarily be for an exchange of materials and skills that are naturally maldistributed.
- Activities that do not involve financial transactions are no less important than those that do. Consequently there is no justification for the maximization of financial transactions.
- The interests of future generations, and of other communities, must not be jeopardized.

(b) Of Businesses

- The essential purpose of a business is to provide goods and services to meet some of the needs of a defined sector of the market.

- The continuity of a business that is performing satisfactorily in fulfilling its purpose should be protected.
- The well-being of all other stakeholders is as important as that of equity shareholders.
- Through the technologies that are used, operations should enhance the environment rather than damage it, and contribute to ecological balance.
- All forms of waste should be minimized, and renewable energy and materials should be used as much as possible.
- A company does not own all its resources; it holds them in trust to make the best possible use of them on behalf of the community. Therefore it has 'citizenship' responsibilities.
- Managers and employees together are the players in the business game. They should be enabled to participate to the limits of their abilities and have a sense of 'ownership with dignity'.
- Operating units should be kept as small as the maintenance of efficiency allows.
- Companies should be dynamically innovative, striving to achieve higher levels of excellence and quality in all aspects of their business, making the best use of human skills and technologies to that end.
- Investment must place equal weight on the long term as well as the short.
- Company Boards of Directors should be guided by a General Purpose Clause that reflects these assumptions and beliefs.

*Note*: These two lists are not intended to be a dogmatic credo. They are intended only as examples of the assumptions and beliefs that are needed to underpin sustainable development.

1   *Discriminating development*   All who are able and fit to take part in the generation of real wealth – both financial and non-financial – must be enabled to play their part for the benefit of themselves, their families and their local communities. Their activities cannot be indiscriminate. They must be discriminating in the use of resources in order to minimize waste and prevent environmental and ecological damage. Using 'appropriate technologies', wealth generation can be much more evenly spread, fully satisfying all material needs and

opening up a prospect of unlimited development in areas that are not energy- or material-intensive.

2 *Conserving Resources* A clear distinction has to be made between renewable and non-renewable materials and energy sources, with preference being given to renewables wherever possible. There should also be a bias towards locally available resources. Care must be taken to ensure that when renewable materials are taken from the natural stock a balance is maintained by restocking. The ways in which resources are extracted, processed, used and finally disposed of, must be planned with a view to an avoidance of damage to nature and to the maintenance of ecological balance.

> By increasing energy efficiency measures, consumption of energy per unit of GDP could be reduced in the UK by 60% at least by 2025.
>
> *Gerald Leach*[6]

3 *Maximize repair, reconditioning, reuse and recycling (4Rs)* Consumption of virgin materials and manufacturing energy will be minimized if things are designed for maximum durability and repairability. Full advantage of those qualities can be realized if the 4 R services are used to the full.

4 *Creative work* Work should be organized in a variety of ways to make the fullest possible use of human talents and energy in the satisfaction of all kinds of human needs. Technology used by people in their work should be skill enhancing and 'user friendly'. People in employment should be able to identify with it and with its purposes.

5 *Non-material growth* Although material growth has to be limited within the bounds of sustainability, no such limitations need apply to those forms of human activity and personal or community development that need not be material- or energy-intensive (e.g. health care, the arts, social services, sport, hobbies, education).

6 *Self-directed personal investment* To enable discriminating development to take place, opportunities must be available for people to direct their savings into investments that will facilitate such a development. In effect this will mean placing money primarily to serve the needs of individuals and communities, rather than making these needs serve a financial purpose which may or may not accord with the wishes of individual investors or the needs of their community.

| *Unsustainable Development* | *Sustainable Development* |
| --- | --- |
| Indiscriminate development | Discriminating development |
| Unconstrained use of resources and the environment | Resource conservation and care for the environment |
| Maximization of manufacture | Maximization of the 4 Rs |
| Unskilled work | Creative work |
| Maximization of material growth | Maximization of non-material growth |
| Impersonal investment | Self-directed investment |

## Sustainable Development Accentuates the Positive

One way to contrast the overall meaning of these two forms of development is to say that it is a moral choice between 'eat, drink and be merry for tomorrow we die' and 'let us live responsibly now so that others may also live in the future'. This formulation immediately seems like a straight jacket. It actually means being liberated, because the positive aspects greatly outweigh the negative.

For businesses, which are the main agents of economic development, the negative aspects may sound like bad news. It may seem like the denial of freedom to invent and innovate in any way that can be commercialized. It is, of course, inevitable that old things must give way to new in any fundamental change. We shall have to stop doing certain things. However much we might personally regret such constraints, they become entirely acceptable once we remember that they are not arbitrary. It is an imperative placed upon us if life on the planet is to continue with any kind of dignity. In the words used by Margaret Thatcher to the UN General Assembly in November 1989, 'it must be growth which does not plunder the planet today and leave our children with the consequences tomorrow.' Happily, as we shall see later, the positive aspect, which is dominant, opens up marvellous new opportunities.

Sustainable development challenges the entire industrial and commercial system to restructure itself, based on a completely new set of assumptions and beliefs about the ways we must conduct our economic affairs. We should be making a profound mistake if we perceived the change in terms less fundamentally radical than that. Some may be tempted to think that sustainable development means little more than insulating our houses, fitting catalytic mufflers to our cars and buying so-called 'green' produce from the supermarket. That would be for change to continue along conventional lines leaving all the erroneous beliefs and assumptions untouched. The effect would be so marginal as to have little influence on the future of life on the planet, other than to delay the consequences for a generation or so. The magnitude of the per capita reduction in the consumption of fossil energy and non-renewable materials that is needed long-term in the industrialized nations cannot be achieved by tinkering with the problem. A reduction to about one-third of present levels of consumption is required in Europe for sustainability; in the USA it is considerably greater.

The challenge that sustainable development poses to the world's business community must be taken up in its entirety, and at a level of basic assumptions and beliefs. Only in this way can the business sector hope to prove that it is feasible. As the President of the International Chamber of Commerce says,[7] the onus of proof rests with the business sector because it alone controls most of the technological and productive capacity that is needed to bring it about.

The future of sustainable development is one of intense innovation – inventing a new and different age. Innovation will be in the lead, with administration playing its supporting role of serving the needs of people and the planet. It is a prospect full of opportunity for dynamic management.

> We have reached a stage in human development where our future technological progress must be based to an increasing degree on the rational needs of our civilisation rather than let our civilisation be driven about aimlessly by haphazard invention.
>
> *The Duke of Edinburgh*[8]

## Radical Business Transformation Strategies

An effective approach to this new age of opportunity requires not only dynamic management of innovation, but also a radical transformation in a number of critical areas of business life. Figure 1.1 lists nine such

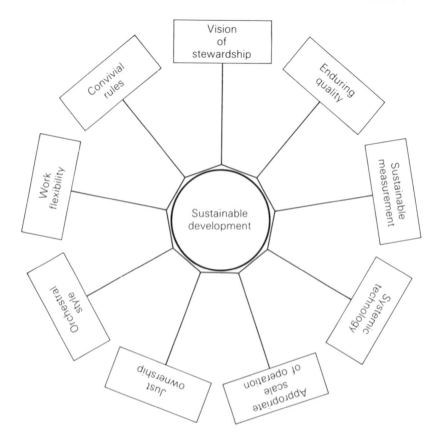

**Figure 1.1**  Transformation strategies for sustainable development.

areas for which sustainable development has vitally important implications. Before considering each in detail in later chapters, we need first to see in what ways there are connections with sustainability arising out of the new set of assumptions and beliefs.

## Vision of Stewardship

For some time it has been widely recognized that companies benefit from published 'mission statements'. Those that have been in existence for the past two decades would, in the majority of cases, place emphasis on developing the business to obtain growth and a high return on the investment of equity shareholders within a defined product or service sector. When development was constrained only by the limits set by the legal system, no more needed to be said to indicate recognition of other forms of restraint, such as those arising from the need to conserve certain types of material or plant species. When the quality of goods or services to be marketed was mentioned, reference might be made to the aim of being leaders in performance, style or fashion, and perhaps to reliability and value for money. Seldom would there have been an explicit expression of ambition to be leaders in durability, repairability or energy efficiency. There might have been an intention to be a dynamic and innovative company, but it is unlikely that any reference would have been made to the motivation for dynamism and innovation, or to the 'stewardship' obligations of the company for the general well-being and to the communities in which it operated. For many years there have been such expressions of corporate social responsibility in a small number of organizations, but they have been the exceptions.

Generally speaking conventional mission statements have been narrowly written. The visions they have embodied have failed to suggest a vital and responsible engagement in a creative endeavour necessary for the general benefit. A company lives not only by its mission statement; it also operates with a set of common values. They vary somewhat from company to company, but in general they reflect the conventional underlying common beliefs and assumptions of trade and industry. The radical change arising out of the moral choice to pursue a course of sustainable development must result in a change both in the shared values and in the vision of most commercial enterprises.

Two examples may serve to illustrate, in part, the relevance of 'vision and values' to sustainable development. The vision of the public electricity supply industry has been a narrow one: that of delivering power reliably at minimum unit cost to customers every hour of the day and every day of the year. If its vision had been different, to remain a reliable source of supply, but to make maximum use of renewable sources of energy and only where necessary to use a fossil fuel input, it would have been an entirely different business. Had the vision gone further and anticipated that generation from fossil fuels would be carried out in combination with generation of heat wherever that was taking place, it would have been even more different.

The domestic heating business is the second example. The conventional approach is for each competing fuel supplier to seek to maximize the volume of sales of fuel to customers. Although advice on efficiency of use may be available on request, the decision whether or not to improve it is left with the householder. If, however, the supply company had a vision of providing customers with a comfortable indoor environment temperature at minimum cost, instead of simply supplying a product, the business would not be the same at all.

Each of the alternative visions of these two illustrations would accord with the kind of approach needed for sustainable development. The value systems underpinning these visions would also be different.

## Appropriate Scale of Operation

Sustainable development raises questions about the nature of business operations, not least about size. The many influences that have been at work over the past century have tended towards increasing the scale of operation in almost every sector. The finance and investment system has been a very big influence, but the main justification for the increase has been that so-called economies of scale make it inevitable. Nevertheless, managers in these big organizations are well aware of the difficulties that size and complexity create. One of the most serious problems for any company that has to be intensely innovative is the inertia a large organization experiences in making rapid responses to the need for frequent change.

Since a change of direction towards sustainable development necessarily means that innovation in all kinds of business will become more intense, it is important to consider carefully the optimum size of operation once the top management has made a commitment to change direction.

The food processing and distribution industries provide a good example of the ways in which a re-examination of the size factor could produce movement towards sustainable development. Over many decades a very fragmented system has been replaced by a concentrated and capital-intensive industrial system based on big processing plants and a massive international distribution system. It appears that when he was Chairman of the Cadbury Schweppes Group, Sir Adrian Cadbury made a careful study of what was required for the future. He came to the conclusion that the historic process needed to be reversed. Siccolt Mansholt, one of the architects of the European Common Agricultural Policy, has studied the primary food production end of the business. His conclusion has much in common with Sir Adrian Cadbury's. He has been quoted as saying that large-scale, energy- and chemical-intensive agriculture has been a mistake, and that quite different and more environmentally harmonious forms of farming need to replace it – another reversal of a historic trend!

## Sustainable Measurement

Every company's management is equipped with a set of measuring instruments for planning, monitoring and controlling the business and its future development. Some of the measurements are common to all businesses. For example, every company needs to know the annual return on the average capital employed. Other measurements are specific to particular kinds of business. The important criterion of sales revenue per square metre of shelf space in a supermarket is obviously of no interest to the manager of a coal mine. Neither is the latter's interest in the hourly output per metre of coal-face of any interest to a supermarket manager.

All of the various measurements that play a vital part in the daily lives of managers have been devised to provide the kind of information they require to run their businesses in accordance with the assumptions and beliefs about what is important and unimportant in economic life in general and business life in particular. With a new set of assumptions and beliefs, and a new vision and set of common values for the company that are a basis for sustainability, managers will need to modify some of the numbers they use daily and eliminate others. Some new numbers will need to be introduced. Without such changes a company is likely to continue on a 'business as usual' course, no matter what the expressed intentions to change may be, or how sincerely they are held.

Three examples can illustrate the radical effect that a change in measuring instrument may have. Discounted Cash Flow has been a widely used method of evaluating investment projects. In its very nature it puts less weight on the future than on the present. A sustainable form of development cannot accept that view; an alternative to DCF will have to be found. Unit cost of production is another common number used of most products. To reflect the importance of product durability for sustainable development, consider, for example, the cost per hour of useful life of electric light bulbs; if this replaced unit costs of bulbs, products of higher first cost would perhaps be produced. If the vision of the manufacturer also aimed to produce bulbs that minimized electricity consumption, a still different kind of bulb would be produced. The third example concerns the building industry and could have even more dramatic effects. One of the traditional, principal objectives in building construction is to minimize first cost. In so doing buildings have been produced which are vastly more inefficient thermally than they need be. Had 'total cost of construction, maintenance and operation over a 50 year period' been used as an alternative criterion for minimization a very different stock of buildings would be in existence.

Numbers that are used in businesses will be crucially important for sustainable development.

## Work Flexibility

Kinds of work re-arrangements that are likely to be beneficial for intensely innovative activity are already taking place in some companies. The monolithic, entirely self-reliant, hierarchical form is being replaced by multi-dimensional arrangements. These are capable of great flexibility and adaptability. They leave as many options open as possible for coping with uncertainty. The potential of Information Technology will enable the new arrangements, with their looser non-bureaucratic systems, to cope effectively.

New work arrangements will have to do more than merely provide greater flexibility and freedom for managements. They will have to take full account of the changing expectations and attitudes of a work-force that is increasingly composed of a variety of specialist skills. The marriage of business needs with the needs of the work-force will frequently produce companies with small core operations that employ, on contract terms, the services of a cluster of specialist suppliers of skill, knowledge, technology and effort.

A comparison of the old MG car company and the Morgan car company provides an illustration of different work arrangements in the same business of sports car manufacture; one was a traditional monolithic firm doing itself as much of the job of designing and manufacturing as it could, whereas the other concentrated on design and final assembly on a low-capital, high-labour basis, with much of the manufacture being contracted out. Lord Nuffield chose to use much the same kind of high-capital production system for his sports cars as he used for the mass-market, popular Morris models. Morgan chose to use a much less capital-intensive system, with a small, highly skilled and enthusiastic team of production workers for the small volume production job, relying on their design skills to fill a particular market niche. Morgan still has a healthy business with its well-adapted organization of work; MG was unfortunately forced to cease trading some years ago.

Not only is more and more work being sub-contracted. Some companies will increasingly benefit if some of their in-house 'core' activity is carried out by employees working from home rather than from a company plant or office.

## Orchestral Style

In the best companies autocratic and paternalistic management styles have been gradually changing to more consultative forms. With the emergence of 'total quality management' a further advance is being made towards greater participation at all levels.

The challenge of sustainable development requires that movement towards a participative style of management should accelerate in all kinds of company. The principal reason is that 'man management' becomes an even more critical factor than it has ever been. Comparatively small teams of highly skilled professionals in a wide variety of specialisms can only be led successfully with the kind of leadership – such as is displayed by the conductor of an orchestra – that inspires full participation. Management of multi-disciplinary R&D teams provides a useful business model in which a similar kind of leadership is practised.

It is not uncommon to find such styles of management in some computer software companies. It is mistaken to think that similar leadership is inappropriate in more traditional forms of business, with their different history of organizational development. Changing styles in such companies, from autocracy to participation, is not an easy job. Happily there are examples where it has been achieved very successfully. One outstanding example is discussed in chapter 7. Before it was converted into a Partnership Company, the Baxi Heating Company was a traditional family firm, founded in the 19th century to make a patent coal fire system. When the business was taken over by Philip Baxendale, the grandson of the founder, he began to encourage participation. As a result the firm became increasingly successful and prosperous as an innovator in the domestic gas heater business. Philip Baxendale believes that participation made a big contribution to the success.

## Just Ownership

An 'absentee landlord' system of ownership that came into existence with the invention of the joint stock limited liability company has become the dominant form of ownership in free-market economies during an era of indiscriminate economic growth. Unconstrained investment and indiscriminate growth were well matched. Discriminating growth for sustainable development requires responsible, long-term investment from sources that have both a vested interest in the corporate agent and a legal obligation to serve the common good as well as the stakeholders. The 'absentee landlord' system, as it presently operates, is not best suited to that role; alternative forms of ownership need to be promoted.

There are other practical reasons, but there is also an important moral consideration. The choice being made for sustainability is based on principles of natural justice and equity. For this choice to be effectively pursued similar principles must be employed within the agencies that are engaged in the task. Thus businesses must be seen to be operating on just and equitable principles. This requires some fundamental changes in the dominant company law covering joint stock limited liability. To use George Goyder's term,[9] we need just enterprises.

Examples of different ownership structures already in existence may be useful conversion models. The Baxi Partnership is an attractive model for any family company contemplating a change of ownership. The Body Shop and other franchising examples point the way to alternatives that, to a greater or lesser extent, decentralize control and obligation, thereby creating a closer relationship between investment and a particular small group of workpeople. Although employee and management buy-outs have become more common in recent years, and will probably continue to increase, the main part of the private-company sector is likely to remain substantially intact. A major change in company law will be needed to bring about a more just relationship between employer and employee, and restore an element of public benefit accountability and linkage between ownership obligations and rights.

## Enduring Quality

Some of the things that are happening in the food production, processing and distribution industries illustrate how environmental issues and product quality are inseparable. Farming is beginning to undergo a major reformation. Processing is rapidly having to switch from additives, and marketers are suddenly faced with customer demands for biodegradable and recyclable packages. Processes themselves are under public scrutiny; for example, the radiation treatment of foods and the chlorine whitening of paper products are being questioned.

The value changes that are both explicit and implicit in a move towards sustainability will have profound effects on the meaning of quality and its expression. Across the entire business spectrum the concepts of quality are likely to undergo very many changes, from the rather narrow contemporary concept to questions of resources and environment, new codes of good practice and new standards for managers and professionals.

The implications of sustainability for business professional Codes and Standards are considerable. For example, the main constraints that professional engineers have traditionally insisted on have been concerned with health and safety, together with compliance with minimum standards required by official regulations. Construction engineers and architects have for a very long time had the know-how to erect buildings requiring only a fraction of the space-heating energy used in existing buildings. Automotive engineers have had the know-how to design cars that would use about half the amount of fuel consumed at present, and which would also last two or three times as long. The imperative of sustainability will surely add maximization of durability, repairability and energy efficiency to health and safety, as things that professional codes require.

## Convivial Rules

The rules that govern the operation of businesses have been designed to foster the indiscriminate growth that is leading towards environmental and ecological damage of global proportions and the rapid exhaustion of some non-renewable resources. They have also led to concepts of quality, types of technology, instruments of business management and systems of corporate ownership that appear to be inappropriate in a period of discriminating economic growth.

The business game rules obviously reflected the old assumptions and beliefs that were listed earlier in this chapter. For example, on the grounds of so-called economies of scale, it was believed that there would be natural advantage in linking large-scale marketing with large-scale manufacturing operations. According to that belief it would obviously be disadvantageous to interfere, through official regulations, by restraining the discount that a retailing chain might obtain from a manufacturer for a nation-wide, big-volume contract for a particular product. Similarly, the same generalized belief in economies of scale rules out interference in all but a very few examples of company take-over.

Under a new set of assumptions and beliefs about what principles must apply if sustainable development is to be achieved, existing rules of business must be carefully reviewed and tested against the new principles. If 'horses for courses' is to replace 'the bigger the better' in the optimization of size of operation there may be cases in which limitation of discounts and restraint on take-overs would be beneficial.

### Systemic technology

From what has already been said in previous sections, technological development will be transformed by a decision in favour of sustainability. Technology is by no means neutral. It serves whatever purpose we expect of it. It can be an immense contributor to good; or it can be frighteningly destructive. The peaceful purposes for which we have so far used it have done much good, but unwittingly it has been the direct cause of the serious environmental and ecological threat. It is clear that, in future, much more careful attention will have to be paid to any new technological developments. In particular, all possible side-effects will need to be studied in great detail before widespread use is allowed. However, if development objectives are embodying principles of sustainability, side-effects should not be a big problem. The new developments will not only be about things that have never been done before. By far the majority will be ways of doing most of the common things that fulfil human needs and wants, but in ways that serve the new purpose of sustainable development. This makes the challenge to scientists, technologists and engineers very widespread and very profound.

In two particular ways the change is revolutionary. Since the beginning of the Industrial Revolution the process of development has become increasingly fragmented as knowledge and experience have accumulated and individuals have become more specialized. As a result the focus of attention has tended to be on the achievement of progressive improvements in elements of the total system. For example, much effort has been put into the development of better and more efficient domestic heating appliances. Unfortunately too little attention was paid to the thermal design of the complete building, with the result that most of the space-heat continues to be wasted. The result would have been quite different with a 'systems approach' to development rather than the traditional 'blinkered approach'. Instead of maximizing the performance of one element of the system, we would have optimized the whole system. For the future the process of fragmentation in development needs to be reversed. A 'systems approach' has become increasingly necessary.

> Early in the next century the world for the first time will be distributing a shortage instead of a surplus of a vital commodity energy, unless . . .
>
> *J. Kiely*[10]

A second revolutionary change concerns the types of material and the sources of energy that we use. The first Industrial Revolution was based on a switch from renewable wind, water and wood to non-renewable fossil fuels as sources of energy. It also depended on the use of an expanding range of highly-processed, non-renewable materials in place of natural materials. For example, synthetic fibres have to a considerable extent replaced natural fibres. Synthetic alcohol based on petroleum feedstocks has taken over much of the market previously supplied by fermentation alcohol. Plastic materials have displaced paper products in some types of packaging. In the second Industrial Revolution, as we seek to contain environmental and ecological damage whilst making space for an improvement in the living conditions of three-quarters of the world's population, the recent historic process will need to be reversed by using more renewables.

## Summary

Recognition of the necessity of a form of development that is sustainable demands a fundamental break from some of the important assumptions and beliefs that have underpinned traditional development since the beginning of the Industrial Revolution. A new set of assumptions and beliefs will be needed to guide development towards sustainabiity. Success or failure depends primarily on businesses which have control over the human skills and the material, financial and technological resources that are capable of effecting the change.

Sustainable development is a complex idea which, from a business point of view, can be described as something that (a) uses renewable resources in preference to non-renewables, (b) uses technologies that are environmentally harmonious, ecologically stable and skill enhancing, (c) designs complete systems in order to minimize waste, (d) reduces as much as possible the consumption of scarce resources by designing long-life products that are easily repairable and can be recycled and (e) maximizes the use of all the services that are not energy- or material-intensive, but which contribute to the quality of life.

All of this profoundly challenges companies everywhere and at all levels. Nine re-orientations in business life are required. They are towards

1  a corporate vision of stewardship;
2  an appropriate scale of operation;
3  the measuring of sustainability;
4  flexible work arrangements;
5  an orchestral style of management;
6  enduring quality;
7  just forms of ownership;
8  convivial rules of the business game;
9  systemic technology.

Each involves a separate task for a company, out of which a transformation programme should be produced. Although, inevitably, there are new constraints, these are more than offset by the vast range of new opportunities to be seized by imaginative firms in a period of intense innovation.

There can be no generalized solutions. The chapters that follow address the specific problems and opportunities that need to be resolved in each area of sustainable development. They provide the necessary guidelines for dealing constructively with the most basic changes that have faced businesses for 200 years, the outcome of which will literally determine the future of the human race and the planet.

## Notes

\* J. Harvey-Jones, *Making it Happen – Reflections on Leadership*, Collins, 1988.

1 E. F. Schumacher, *Small is Beautiful*.

2 *A Matter of Degrees*, a research report by the President of the World Resources Institute, 1989.

3 *Global 2000 Report*, prepared for the President of the United States by the Department of State and the Council for Environmental Policy, 1980.

4 *Our Common Future*, the Brundtland Report. World Commission on Environment and Development, 1988.

5 F. Hirsch, *Social Limits to Growth*. Routledge & Kegan Paul, 1977.

6 G. Leach, *A Low Energy Strategy for the UK*. Science Reviews Ltd., 1979.

7 P. Wallenberg, President of the International Chamber of Commerce. *Sustainable Development – the Business Approach*. ICC, Stockholm, 1989.

8 HRH The Duke of Edinburgh, The Melchett Lecture of the Institute of Fuel. London, 1967.

9 G. Goyder, *The Just Enterprise*. André Deutsch, 1987.

10 J. Kiely, 4th Wilson Campbell Memorial Lecture.

# 2

# Vision and Values

Where there is no vision people perish.

*Proverbs* 29

We need a fresh vision of business enterprise.

George Goyder*

The kaleidoscope of basic changes described in the previous chapter, which are symptoms of the present paradigm shift, arise from the gradual transformation of vision and values that permeate society. Business is part of society and will also experience the transformation of its own vision and values. The task of management throughout this period of uncertainty is nothing less than to 'invent the future'. Responding belatedly to unexpected changes will not do. Management has to be innovative; and the key to successful innovation is a clear vision that is communicated daily in word and deed, reinforced by a well-understood and agreed set of shared values throughout the company.

## Visions of Essential Purpose

Visions can motivate; but they can also have the reverse effect. The notion that the fundamental purpose of a business is to make money is one that I grew up with. It was not until 1957, when I attended a seminar of about a dozen marketing managers from different countries, that I gave it conscious consideration. At one point in the meeting we were all asked to express personal views as to the fundamental purposes of our various companies. Each manager spoke in turn and I happened to be last. As I listened to the others, they all

in their different ways seemed to be saying that the essential purpose
of their companies was to make money; as much of it as possible.
When it came to my turn I found myself – to my amazement, as I later
reflected on the discussion – saying that, of course, it must be
nonsense to say that our essential purpose was to make money.
Clearly our companies had to add value (make money) in order to pay
salaries, wages and other bills, and to generate an adequate profit to
satisfy shareholders and other suppliers of finance; but this was a
means to an end – a necessary condition of survival and healthy growth
– not an essential purpose of the enterprise. 'That essential purpose',
I said, 'has to be the complete satisfaction of all the needs of
customers and potential customers relating to our product and
service. Making money can no more be a purpose than breathing is
the purpose of life. Both are conditions of survival; means and not
ends.' The strange thing about the ensuing discussion was that it was
as though I had been guilty – albeit inadvertently – of a heresy that
might undermine the foundations of free enterprise.

This feeling came to me again more than twenty years later when
the same topic (the essential purpose of business) was being discussed
with a small group of very senior bankers. On this occasion their
reaction was even stronger. The marketing managers had been able
without difficulty to accept that their products and services were
central to their enterprises. The bankers on the other hand appeared
to have little or no interest in what money was *for*. Money alone had
pre-eminence for them. Everything else had to serve the purpose of
money; although they had accepted that it was mostly necessary to
satisfy customers in the interests of money. The basic idea on which I
had endeavoured to gain their agreement – that the customer alone is
pre-eminent amongst all others concerned with a business – was
totally rejected.

Shortly before that meeting with bankers I was discussing careers
with a group of sixth-formers and their teachers from an inner-city
school. When I suggested that they should look upon business as the
primary social service that generates the resources, both material and
financial, that are used by the social services, their teachers protested
very strongly. Businesses, in their perception, existed to make money
for proprietors and shareholders. They could not accept that there
was a social purpose that they pre-eminently served.

One way of looking at these differences of perception is to say that
they are rather academic and philosophical and of no real practical

significance. This view greatly underestimates their importance in at least two very important ways, which are becoming increasingly critical with the passage of time. First, there is the survival necessity of a total customer orientation in every part of a business. Second, there is the equally necessary practical recognition that highly motivated, skilled and committed people make a company successful. A business is *for* people *by* people.

No matter what protestations a company may make about its desire to satisfy customers, if each customer is seen as merely the object of a money-making exercise, the protestations will certainly be recognized for what they are – hollow. Given the choice of dealing with other companies that genuinely do what they say, putting the interests of customers first, there is no doubt which way the business will go. Similarly, no matter how much and how often the top management of a company may acknowledge that it is the people in the company who must have credit for its success, if, in practice, greater attention is paid to money than to people, the company will lose; because the people will not be deceived. Their potential as creative, intelligent and energetic individuals, who are at their best when cooperating in teams, will not be realized. It is highly misguided idealism on the part of senior managements that leads them to expect that employees can be motivated by the notion of making money for unknown shareholders.

It is bad enough for managers in private, and amongst themselves, to be expressing to each other the notion that they are in business to make money for their shareholders, but frequently, regardless of the audience, the same purpose is proudly expressed publicly. It sometimes seems as though there is an aggressive competition to enrich faceless shareholders. Of course, the shareholders must be satisfied with their investment; the business needs them. They are essential contributors, as are all other stakeholders. They help to satisfy the needs of customers with goods and services; and they are no less important simply because they are a means and not the essential purpose of the business itself. Yet the consequences, for motivation and public regard, of changing the tune could be dramatic, if it was publicly declared, and constantly demonstrated, that companies are unreservedly in business for the sole purpose of serving their customers. Whatever else may be part of the vision of a company as it is perceived by both insiders and the rest of society, the manifestation of its essential purpose is fundamental.

## A Rolls Royce Vision

There is more to the vision than is portrayed. Rolls Royce employed me as an engineering apprentice in 1940. I applied to them rather than to any other company, even though I knew that my lodgings would absorb all my pay, because I believed that its engineering – particularly its Merlin aero-engine – was the best in the world. I felt it an honour to be accepted for training by the best engineers in the best engineering. How many people have the satisfaction of feeling themselves honoured to be employed because they are joining a company that strives to be the best in its particular field of activity? My perception was no doubt a little naive, as I discovered when I began to clock in. Nevertheless, even though I joined at the height of the Battle of Britain, and it seemed as if every extra engine that could be produced for Spitfires and Hurricanes might determine the outcome of the war, there was never any question of sacrificing any aspect of quality for quantity. Sir Henry Royce had died years earlier but his spirit and striving after excellence still dominated the atmosphere, and the highest standards of work were maintained despite the pressure to produce more.

Many impressions were made on me which I have valued and retained. A man I worked with in the heat treatment shop provided me with one of them. I was profoundly impressed by the care and concentration that he showed as he measured the surface hardness of gears. It was, I thought, a rather dull repetitive job that he worked at day in and day out. I knew him to be a very intelligent man, and I was puzzled by his ability to maintain such a high degree of concentration and dedication to the job. When I asked him to explain how he managed it, he simply smiled and said 'Don't you realise that if I make a mistake and pass an off-grade single gear it may cost some poor young pilot his life.' Here was a man who looked beyond the chunk of steel to the person who was to make use of it, who would be affected by his work. This was my first realization that engineering is about people and not only about things. Later experience as an Engineer Officer in the Fleet Air Arm, maintaining and repairing Seafire Merlin engines, helped reinforce the conviction that engineering is about people most of all and the Rolls Royce dictum that only the best is good enough.

## A Shell Vision

Joining Shell as a Research Engineer, on leaving the Navy, I was fortunate for the second time to be in a company that was fiercely jealous of its reputation for the quality of its products and service. When, a few years later, I was responsible for world-wide quality standards of Shell petroleum products, I required no guidance as to where our products must be in the league table of product quality and service. My appointment to that responsibility in the mid 1950s coincided with a fundamental change whereby the marketing function was held accountable for product development in order to reinforce customer orientation and stimulate innovation.

My personal conviction about the priority of people in engineering and technology found an immediate outlet. The lessons learned in Rolls Royce and the Royal Navy were a key influence in a radically different approach to quality management. In answer to the question 'How did product specifications come to be the way they are?' the general answer seemed to be that they grew randomly in the light of experience over the years. The next question was 'What influence does the users' appreciation have on the choice of control parameters and the setting of levels?' The answer was that there had been no direct influence. The choices had been made on 'technical considerations'; for after all 'it was the machines that were the real users of our petroleum products.' 'In any case, customers seem happy enough and we get very few complaints.' What I could not find out was the extent to which customers might respond to a change in particular control parameters. It was important that I should know because if a product property change, which cost very little, was well appreciated – for example by car drivers – it might provide a basis for a marketing initiative. On the other hand, if the level of the freeze point of a diesel fuel was set too low to be of benefit to the user, a good deal of money might be saved by the elimination of a gratuitous quality give-away.

So we set to work to find out what changes in product properties were noticed by our human customers as well as by the machines in which they were used. There were some very surprising results that caused us to make some important changes. Not only did this provide welcome improvements for many of our customers who we knew were feeling a real benefit; but also we were able to offer our refinery colleagues savings and greater flexibility in their operations. We estimated that one such change alone was worth about £12m per annum on a world-wide basis. Another important lesson learned from this 'customer reaction trial' approach to product specification was that ordinary people are sometimes capable of detecting changes that laboratory instruments are unable to identify. We first suspected this when a minute change that was only just measurable in a laboratory test was noticed by about 30 per cent of motorists. It became a *cause célèbre* with the launch of the Ignition Control Additive (ICA) in the early 1950s. Not only did the additive cure the problems of spark-plug fouling for which it was originally designed, but it was also more widely welcomed by the motoring public for other benefits that they detected. As a result it was a much greater marketing success than could be expected on the basis of laboratory work. It is paradoxical how, when asked by market researchers if they think there are any differences between one oil company's fuel and another's, motorists will nearly always individually say No, yet, when a carefully planned 'customer reaction trial' is carried out, similar to those used for drugs by the medical profession, they frequently demonstrate that they are aware of differences. The positive driver experience is reflected in tests of brand choice in a multi-brand motorway service station where all other things are equal except for brand of product.

The vision of Shell differs from and is in some ways more complex than those of other oil companies. Various oil industry authors have identified them with a distinctive management style. It is a style with a light touch that succeeds in maintaining a strong family sense in the many different Shell national operating companies whilst at the same time allowing considerable variety and diversity. When the London/Hague Head Offices were transformed in 1959 into the London/Hague Service Company Offices, a fundamental process of devolution and decentralization began that turned the Shell 'Group' into an extraordinary and truly international group of companies of all nationalities. It was Professor Parkinson, of Parkinson's law, who once remarked publicly that if you wanted to see nationals of all colours and creeds working harmoniously together you could see it at its best in Shell companies around the world. I do not recall ever seeing an example of discrimination because of nationality, race or religion.

Apart from the important influence of individual senior managers in creating the family atmosphere, over many years, I believe that the sensitive way in which personnel matters were handled at all levels was an important contributory factor. Manuals provided sufficient but not too much regulation, but all levels of management were given plenty of scope for exercising personal judgement in dealing with individuals. Inevitably this resulted in some variation in the treatment of people, and this occasionally gave rise to annoyance. On the whole most people felt that there was a good degree of fairness exercised. I believe that most preferred to feel that each person was treated as a special individual having unique personal circumstances rather than merely as a unit in a particular job category.

Another factor that must have contributed to the vision and image of the company was the long history of corporate participative citizenship that was manifested in many different ways. Just one of several examples with which I had some contact was the Shell Film Unit. Certainly it made some films that were obviously promotional by nature. Others were made, such as one concerned with the basic principles of flight, that were simply a contribution to education. The only thing that revealed its origins was the credits at the beginning and the end.

This creation and sustaining of a vision, an ethos and an atmosphere was for a very long time an entirely informal affair. It evolved through the interplay of people, their perceptions and beliefs with the environment and circumstances of each particular period. It was not until the mid 1960s that the need to write down some kind of company philosophy was felt. The process of preparing such an important statement is well described by Paul Hill.[1] For me the most remarkable aspect concerned the trustee relationship felt towards the resources that it was using for the benefit of society, though there were also other expressions of corporate social responsibility. This became of special significance to me in 1977, after I had retired from Shell and was in the middle of trying to help set up some of the first local enterprise trusts with companies like Pilkingtons of St Helens, the Mond Division of ICI and various other commercial and industrial firms. In his Ashridge Lecture, the late C. C. Pocock, who was then Chairman of Shell, spoke of his belief that 'big companies should establish a positive management policy which recognises the value of small enterprises . . . and resolve to support this in action.'[2] Since then a great many big companies have, among their other expressions of corporate responsibility, done a great deal to put that belief into action. As a result there are over 300 local enterprise trusts and agencies in the UK. In his book Paul Hill stated that there were marked improvements in employee and management attitudes which in the main stemmed from the interactive process of preparing the statement of shared beliefs and values.[3]

## A Johnson & Johnson Vision

In 1980, when I was called in to see how Johnson & Johnson might play a part in a new employment initiative in Surrey, I was shown a copy of their 'Company Credo', which was first given to employees in the United States in 1947. Twenty-eight years later the Chairman, Jim Burke, became concerned that they may not be practising what they preached. He set up a 'Credo Challenge Meeting' with twenty-four senior managers from around the world. At that meeting they discovered that there was far more power in their guiding principles document than they had ever imagined. More such meetings followed, annually, and the dry bones of a seemingly pretentious creed came to life in changed company behaviour. Such published statements are very powerful weapons when seriously put to use. But they are a two-edged sword. If they are published and *not* acted upon they bring scorn and derision on the company, not only from the outside world, but also from employees who regard them as proof of a lack of management integrity. When that happens the most essential of all relationships between employees and management – mutual trust and confidence – is lost. It cannot be regained without a change of management. (For the Johnson & Johnson Credo see page 207.)

## A Sony Vision

The vision of the Sony electronics company is extraordinary. It appears to be something like the visions of all who sought to go beyond whatever had been previously achieved. In their case it is a vision of being the advance frontier – or beyond – of electronic technology application, not once or even for a short while, but for all the time. In a society in which company loyalty and group effort are most highly valued, the two Sony founders, Ibuka and Morita, place most value on individual creativity. They know that their vision would be a mirage without a company of extraordinarily creative individuals. They have had to reject the idea of making people fit jobs. The job has to be tailored to make best use of an employee's unique qualities. Since they take such pride in recruiting people of extraordinary variety the task of matching jobs to people must be extremely difficult. The Sony vision must call for very remarkable innovative management; but something of the kind may very well be required in more companies of the New Age.


## A Body Shop Vision

There is another and very different kind of vision. It is a vision which in many ways is expressive of the closing decade of the twentieth century. It is one that has inspired Anita Roddick's very successful Body Shop chain of franchised retail stores – about 300 in 30 different countries. She puts it into a couple of sentences. Speaking of her own business, and business in general, she says 'We must put back into society what we have taken out. And if we don't love our staff, our neighbours, the environment, we'll be doomed. I want it to be attractive to be good.' It certainly seems to be a vision that works well by any criteria. All Body Shop products come from natural ingredients. They are packaged in recycled paper, reusable bottles or biodegradable containers. Everything is done with honesty and openness.

Pinned in Roddick's office is a slogan: 'We WILL be the most honest cosmetic company. Full Stop.' Although she is a human dynamo and, according to her husband, a 'volcano of creativity', she is determined that the business must be as human and caring as possible. This does not stop at staff, managers, suppliers and customers. Caring extends to community projects. Every shop is required to have one. They do not simply make charitable donations: staff are personally involved. At the wider international level, direct trade with Third World grass-roots suppliers – with no middlemen involved – is high on the Body Shop agenda. She calls it 'New Age thinking'.

> Progress is not just being faster and noisier and bigger; progress is to do with people and the environment in which we live. Progress is not simply a matter of new invention; progress means filling ordinary human needs.
>
> *The Duke of Edinburgh*[4]

The Rolls Royce vision was simple and uncomplicated – nothing but the best was good enough. Shell's was similar in so far as it aimed to be best with its products and services; but it was less elitist, and was sensitive to the needs of a very wide cross-section of the world's population. And it was a vision of an international family that became increasingly complex in response to changing circumstances, such as the new demands for wider consultation and participation, and to growing environmental concerns. The Johnson & Johnson 'credo' was an early attempt to express a concept of general corporate social responsibility set alongside responsibility to stakeholders in the company. Anita Roddick, in her Body Shops, gathers together all the elements embodied in the others, but encourages a degree of autonomy among its individually franchised shops that could make it a prototype for many businesses of the New Age. Her 'family' is a family of independent, adult offsprings scattered throughout the world. In that sense it is unlike the families of subsidiaries of most multinational companies that developed earlier in the century.

## Corporate Values

Where the vision of a company is a living reality in all aspects of its operation, there is a close correspondence between vision and values. However, in this less than perfect world, the values that are manifested in what is done or said by a company are often not so much an accurate reflection of its own vision as of alien values that invade it. The degree to which such alien values are able to infiltrate depends to a very considerable extent upon the conscious effort made by management at all levels to make known the company system of values by word and deed, and to enable colleagues to live and work by them.

If a company senior manager genuinely believes that the complete satisfaction of the needs of customers is the essential purpose of the company, he or she would need to be as concerned as I was when I spent several weeks listening to a very wide range of staff – at all levels – in a company that I will call the Stikfast Company. The real operational value system of a firm does not necessarily correspond with the fine phrases that appear in company manuals. They are to be found in the everyday exchanges of conversation and informal notes that pass between employees and managers. Here are a few examples of the kind of thing that I heard repeatedly as I went round the Stikfast Company.

'This is a fairly labour intensive operation and we have had a good deal of trouble in recent years. I believe we ought to invest in a new greenfield site factory in another locality.'

'The several production plants scattered across the country, each with its own management and administration, must be a costly and inefficient way of doing business. Surely it would be better to replace them with one big central factory.'

'I believe we shall get better productivity if we provide better working conditions. That's where we should spend some money.'

'Looking at the figures, I don't see how we can survive without higher product prices.'

'I don't think we should bother with small accounts. Let's concentrate on the big ones.'

'We used to be sole supplier to Company X: now they are taking deliveries from competitors. I think we ought to give them longer credit and a better discount to win them back.'

'I don't think that department bonuses are much use. I believe individual ones are more effective.'

'I'm not interested in qualitative arguments. What I want are some firm figures.'

'We don't keep a regular record of orders-not-fulfilled five days after order.'

As I reflected on all that I had seen and heard during my investigation I was struck by the fact that, whatever its source, most of the information and advice that I had been given sounded similar. Much of it was about money; furthermore financial solutions were widely felt to provide the answer to the company's financial problems. In so far as non-monetary matters were considered, either their relevance was not understood or they were thought to be distractions. The attitude to people, both inside and outside the company was somewhat negative. The 'unreasonable' demands of customers for things like prompt delivery were a nuisance; and the fewer 'unreasonable' employees the better!

From top to bottom here was an ailing company, which had received several years of 'financial treatment' from a series of Managing Directors and Management Consultants, which continued to believe that its salvation was to be found in a further dose of that treatment. Whatever the Chairman's annual reports said about the vital part that employees played, the real interest and faith was in money rather than in people. The principal concern was inward looking at company performance rather than outward looking at customer orientation – a preoccupation with the excellence of its customer service before and after sale.

It is instructive to compare the action programme that would have followed from the money-orientated value system advice that I had inherited with the people-orientated values that were to underpin the plan that was successfully implemented.

| *Money System* | *People System* |
|---|---|
| 1 Increase product sales prices. | By means of improved efficiency maintain low price. |
| 2 Amalgamate fragmented production units. | Give greater authority to plant managers and trust and encourage them to motivate their people. |
| 3 Make a major new greenfield site investment. | Make changes that motivate managers and workers to operate the existing plant effectively, with a minor investment in improved layout. |
| 4 Develop and introduce a complete new range of products. | Set high standards of quality assurance and delivery. Focus new development on high added value products for high growth markets. |
| 5 Strengthen the sales force. | Reduce the sales force, and give more responsibility and motivation. |
| 6 Maximize sales volume. | Be selective in order to ensure good service where it is most appreciated. |
| 7 Keep manpower costs down. | Be sure that everyone is contributing and is fully involved, committed and well paid. |

It is not possible to say what would have happened had the money system plan been followed. Two years later the market struck a very bad patch. I am inclined to think that if complete failure had not occurred before, it would have occurred then. The benefits of the people system changes were felt quite quickly. Losses were eliminated within a year and by the time the market went sour, good profits were being earned. Fifteen years later the Stikfast Company has continued to do well under several different Managing Directors, each one of whom has built on the same or similar sets of principles and values.

## People as 'Agents' or 'Objects'?

However, there is an important complication about the concept of people-orientated values because there is no single view of 'people at work'. This is well illustrated by two contrasting views prepared by the Work Research Unit of the Department of Employment in London, which it derived from presentations made at the 'Quality of Working Life in the 80s' Conference in Toronto in August 1981. One view was of 'people as objects'; the other was of 'people as agents'. The 'as objects' view regards employees as dispensable factors of production; the 'as agents' view considers them to be a unique resource of remarkable potential. The former view is that an employee is required to fulfil certain functions determined by the technological system, whereas the latter logically concludes that jobs should be designed to allow as much as possible of employees' potential to be realized. The Sony company, mentioned earlier, is a striking example of a 'people as agents' view. Another example comes from an interview with the managing director of a Japanese company manufacturing batteries in South Wales. Asked what his first priority was, the answer was 'People'. He went on to say that they must, of course, be well trained and skilled for the task that they have to perform, but that they must also think and enjoy.

There is a similar, contrasting view of managers. The 'as objects' view is that of a controller with exclusive and absolute rights and authority, such that no initiative may be taken within the organization without express permission. It is not unlike the master–slave relationship. I once succeeded, as occupier of a certain desk, someone who had, unknown to me, operated under that assumption. After a few days in office I realized that the business was merely ticking over under its own momentum. Everyone was waiting for orders to beissued. Had the company been used to seeing people as agents rather than as objects there would have been widespread participation as agents of change and in shared decision-making. The people-orientation that is essential in an age of radical change and uncertainty is undoubtedly one that views people as agents and not as objects.

## People-centred Value Systems

One person's conviction, though based on experience and observation, cannot be wholly convincing. There is something unique and subjective about any individual's experience that does not allow a generalized assertion about the superiority of a system of shared values and beliefs in business that is based on a 'people as agents' perspective. I do not believe that I would be justified in that assertion were it not for weighty independent evidence in support of it. More and more has come to light in the last twenty years, as the new technologies have become established and as public attitudes demand greater democratic choice and participation.

One of the best sources of support for the idea that the nature of shared values and beliefs in an organization is of crucial importance is Peters and Waterman's *In Search of Excellence*.[5] Their studies covered seventy-five highly regarded American companies. They sought to discover what it was that particularly distinguished companies which were outstandingly 'adroit at continually responding to change of any sort in their environments', observing that such companies were most excellent innovators. In their book they say

The [study] project showed, more clearly than could have been hoped for, that excellent companies were, above all, brilliant on the basics. Tools did not substitute for thinking. Intellect didn't overpower wisdom. Analysis did not impede action. Rather these companies worked hard to keep things simple in a complex world. They persisted. They insisted on top quality. They fawned on their customers. They listened to their employees and treated them like adults. They allowed their innovative product and service 'champions' long tethers. They allowed some chaos in return for quick action and regular experimentation.

This summary shows very clearly that these were essentially people-orientated companies and, moreover, that they must have had close correspondence in their whole systems of shared values and beliefs.

**Excellent Innovative Company Characteristics**

This conclusion is reinforced by the eight characteristic attributes possessed by these excellent innovative companies.

1  *Fleet-of-foot*   Instead of having armies of people grinding away endlessly in-house, nervously trying to ensure that all the loose ends have been tied up before the grand world-wide launch, they rely on a few bright people to experiment for a while with cheap prototypes, testing out ideas on a few intimate customers. Although they are big companies, they manage to operate in the same human, organic way that small innovative companies are forced to adopt through lack of resources.

2  *Simple and lean*   The innovative, fleet-of-foot operation is only possible because the company superstructure of top-level executives is kept lean, and the organization structure is simple and flexible.

3  *Autonomy and entrepreneurship*   Innovation springs from free people; it is necessary to have enough of them. They must be on a loose rein. That demands mutual trust and a willingness to accept a reasonable number of mistakes. The time to worry is when none are being made!

4  *Close to customers*   Customers are not out there, separate from the business; they are colleagues, part of it and first among equals. They are served in the supply of products and services. They serve through teaching management precisely what their needs are, and how well they are, or are not, being satisfied. Listening to them is often the spark that fires innovation.

5  *Simultaneous loose–tight properties*   For most managers used to conventional, rigid, hierarchical structures, in which they alone manage and everything is kept under tight control, the foregoing sounds very much like anarchy. The crucial ingredient that ensures that order prevails in the midst of apparent chaos is the determination of top managers to concentrate only on those things that must be centrally determined; as much responsibility and authority as possible is placed wherever it can best be exercised without abdicating their interest in it. Instead of the communication barriers that exist in some traditional companies, there is a lively human interaction between the conductor and the players in the company orchestra.

6  *Stick to the knitting*   One of the great dangers in this anthill of

creativity and innovation is that people are by nature not as single-minded as ants in sticking to a common purpose. The originator of a bright idea that may have little to do with business may not be easily restrained if it begins to develop. An important part of the interaction between the conductor and players is to ensure that everyone is playing the same tune or, as Americans say, that they stick to the knitting and engage only in ventures in which the company has complete competence.

7 *Productivity through people* It is vital that the outcome of innovative activity is carried out efficiently. Excellent, innovative companies know that factories with identical high-investment plant can differ greatly in terms of quality and productivity. The only possible explanation for the difference is *people* and the way that they make use of the equipment provided. The technical equipment makes a high level of productivity possible, but it is the people operating the total system that can make it a reality. Instead of talking about productivity in terms of output per employee, we should express it as a percentage of the potential productivity of the system under perfect conditions of operation. In other words, how well is the system being used by the management?

8 *Hands-on, value driven* There are managers who spend nearly all of their time in the seclusion of their offices, relating only to a few individuals who are directly responsible to them. There are also managers who spend very little of their time in that way. They prefer to be out visiting operational units, R&D laboratories, customers, suppliers, gaining direct knowledge of all kinds. Through their 'walking the floor' they are able continuously to express to employees, in words and actions, the vision and values of the company. But that is a rather too inward-looking perception of management. Peters and Austin's phrase 'Managing by Wandering About' (MBWA)[6] is what is most needed in times of rapid change and uncertainty. It is just as important to feel the pulse of the world in which the company operates as it is to have intimate, direct, personal knowledge of all its departments, and influence over them.

Looking to the future of business, the ability of a company to adapt quickly and harmoniously to an environment that is going through a process of radical change affecting basic beliefs and assumptions – a paradigm change – depends more than ever upon the success of all levels of management in creating and sustaining excellence in innovation. In so far as we try to come to terms with those new beliefs and assumptions, both vision and values will need to reflect them. Roddick's Body Shop is a particularly useful example. Paternalistic, autocratic management is an anachronism. Business is about human relationships. The future of human relationships is mutuality. It is also about using the earth's store of limited resources. They are on loan from future generations and we, both as consumers and producers, have an obligation to put back as much as we take out – to replenish the earth. The principle of sustainable resource use must be built into all activities. There are very strict limits to the quantities of pollutants that the atmosphere, the rivers, the sea and the land will tolerate. Activities need to be reshaped to reflect that fact fully. Lastly, the time has gone when people would tolerate subjugation and dependence. This daily becomes increasingly clear in both capitalist and socialist societies. The communications media have taken the lid off Pandora's box. Nor will people tolerate isolated independence. Community, in every sense of the word, calls for many different forms of solidarity and interdependence. The vision and values of companies that are to prosper through the coming decades will need to reflect all of these things.

## Summary

The change in direction of company activities can only come about smoothly if a thoughtful effort is made to change the vision and value systems so that they conform to the conditions for sustainable development that affect any particular business. The choices made will explicitly recognize the priority of meeting the needs of people, whether they be customers, employees or other contributors to the enterprise. The values systems will be people-centred, and the vision will foster a cooperative excellence in innovation that is sensitive to the necessity of conserving scarce resources, while minimizing waste and environmental or ecological damage. Like Roddick's vision of the Body Shop, it will be conscious of a global community accountability, of a responsibility to put back into society what we have taken out, and, wherever possible, of the need to stay grounded in 'human scale' operating units.

## Notes

\* G. Goyder, *The Just Enterprise.*
1 P. Hill, *Towards a New Philosophy of Management.* Gower Press, 1971.
2 C. C. Pocock, the 1977 Ashridge Lecture. Ashridge Management College, Berkhamsted.
3 P. Hill, *Towards a New Philosophy.*
4 HRH The Duke of Edinburgh, *Men Machines and Sacred Cows.*
5 T. J. Peters and R. H. Waterman, *In Search of Excellence.* Harper & Row, New York, 1982.
6 T. J. Peters and N. Austin, *A Passion for Excellence.* Collins, 1985.

# 3

# Horses for Courses – the Size Factor

> The giants [companies] have been led into misrepresenting that efficiency, mass production, and the division of labour require them to be as big as they are, which is not true. Almost every one of them is as big as it is because it got the means, in one way or another, to swell to enormous size, and took advantage of the unrestrained urge to expand, acquire, absorb, dominate.
>
> T. K. Quinn*

Roddick's Body Shop was identified as a useful example of a company that embodies the vision and values that can best serve the interests of sustainable development. One characteristic that differentiates it from the other examples referred to in chapter 2 is an emphasis on keeping things on a 'human scale' so that interdependence may be a daily experience for customers and people at work. Does the question of a business's size have any bearing on sustainable development?

The twentieth century has seen the growth of business giants in most fields of activity. At the close of the century there is in the capitalist world a high degree of concentration in some industries; aircraft and computers are good examples – each is so dominated by a single company as to be close to a private monopoly. In many others, such as motor cars, domestic electronics or washing powders, the market is dominated by a few giants. To a not inconsiderable extent many small and medium-sized companies depend upon the giants for their existence, as well as to fill gaps in the market that are not attractive to the giants.

More than thirty years after T. K. Quinn wrote of the false claim that giant companies are inescapably necessary, they continue to be justified on the 'economies of scale' theories. Unfortunately many managers have fallen into the trap of believing their own advertising and PR; they are convinced that modern technologies, in particular, demand organizations of ever increasing size. Nevertheless, while their size and economic power is being defended with a variety of rationalizations, many managers strive to transform their monolithic structure into a well-coordinated group of small, vigorous and nearly autonomous units or 'profit centres'. In some of the giants there is very little real, natural affinity between the units; in such a case the giant is in effect an investment company in a variety of enterprises in which it has a controlling share.

There is another misrepresentation in defence of size and power. The claim is made that successful management in one kind of business is transferable to any other business, the perception being that money-management is all that really matters. It may suffice in the short term but it is seldom sufficient for the long run.

## What has been Happening to Size?

At the beginning of this chapter reference was made to the process of concentration in most businesses over many decades. As a result a large percentage of the total is handled by a small number of very large companies. It is not unreasonable to ask whether, and to what extent, we have benefited during the last two or three decades. In 1987 there was published a UK comparison of the typical retail prices that were paid for a range of common household goods in the years 1957 and 1987. A third set of figures was added showing what the prices would have been in 1987 had they been the same in real terms as in 1957, with an allowance made for the RPI inflation effect (see table 3.1). The fourth column in the tabulation shows whether the actual price in 1987 was greater, roughly equal or less than the 1957 price corrected for inflation. It is striking that the biggest gains have been on items which make a small demand on household expenditure – TV sets and washing machines – whereas the biggest adverse trends have been on the more important calls on household income – housing and many foods. Over the same thirty years there has been a considerable increase in average household income which more than offsets the adverse price trends. Consequently those on average or above average incomes are better off in real terms than they were in 1957. Unfortunately a not inconsiderable part of the population, those on pensions or other fixed incomes in particular, whose income has not kept pace with inflation, are significantly worse off.

**Table 3.1**  Comparison of household goods prices in the UK, 1957 and 1987

| Household product | 1957 | 1987 | 1957 adjusted | + more – less |
|---|---|---|---|---|
| Average house | £2,170 | £41,150 | £15,632 | +++ |
| TV set – black and white | £90.00 | £75.00 | £647.00 | ––– |
| Citroën 2CV motor car | £598 | £3,094 | £4,300 | – |
| Washing machine | £66.8.6 | £250 | £477 | –– |
| London–Paris air fare | £15.10.0 | £156 | £111 | ++ |
| 1 lb steak | 5/3½ | £3.50 | £1.90 | ++ |
| 1 lb cod | 2/0 | £2.00 | 72p | +++ |
| 1 lb tomatoes | 1/3 | 57p | 56p | = |
| 1 lb bananas | 1/2 | 40p | 42p | = |
| 1 lb butter | 4/1 | £1.04 | 48p | – |
| 6 eggs | 2/2 | 53p | 78p | – |
| Pint of beer | 1/4 | 78p | 48p | + |
| Bottle of Scotch | £1.13.4 | £7.80 | £9.25 | – |
| Gallon of petrol | 5/0 | £1.60 | £1.79 | – |
| 1 lb potatoes | 3d | 12p | 9p | + |
| 2lb loaf of bread | 7½d | 45p | 22p | ++ |
| Pint of milk | 7d | 25p | 22p | + |
| Letter postage | 3d | 18p | 9p | + |
| Electricity – 1 unit | 1½d | 5.4p | 5.0p | + |

Considering the very big advances that have been made in technological productivity, which should have benefited all in reduced real prices, we are bound to wonder whether a large part of the technological gain may have been lost through the complexities of distribution and the high cost of overheads that are a consequence of concentration into big units. Dennis Gabor[1] was struck by the comparatively small reduction in working hours in the West in relation to the big advances in technological productivity. He suggested that, not only had there been an increase in waste product, but also Parkinson's Law had been in operation with 'Work automatically expanding to fill the time available'. Productive 'tool-pushers', he said, had been replaced by 'paper pushers', whose numbers can grow beyond any limit because they can always give work to one another!

## The 'Real' Scale Effects

As with most generalizations there is some truth in the concept of economies of scale. At the most elementary level there is a geometric truth that is very important for some kinds of business. Take, for example, a storage tank or a container of some kind on a transport vehicle. The quantity of material contained in it is proportional to the cube of dimensions, whereas the amount of material used in its construction is related to the square of dimensions. Consequently, the bigger the capacity the bigger will be the saving in materials of construction: one big tank is a cheaper investment than several small ones. However, even at this most basic level, it is seldom wise to take full advantage of this economy of scale by having only a single container in the company. Should it be out of use for a period, for one reason or another, then the whole company might be brought to a standstill if alternatives cannot quickly and easily be hired. Such a temporary facility may well be available in the case of a container or tank. But in the case of a major power station, for example, there may be no alternative. As their capacities have grown to 1,000 megawatt or more, there has been a steady growth in reserve generating capacity to provide costly cover for a breakdown or major overhaul.

There are other 'physical technical' factors which can yield true economies of scale in some industries and businesses. For example, in the 1960s computers were so big and costly that they were not available to small, free-standing organizations. The development of powerful mini-, micro- and desk-top equipment has eliminated that particular economy of scale.

One important, general factor applies to the minimal viable size of any business unit which has to be financially self-supporting. There is a level of gross profit below which operation is unsustainable. Above that minimum level there are real economies of scale in operation until such time as capacity – in terms of physical, human and financial capacity – becomes a limiting factor. Capacity additions are always finite; consequently the build-up to a new and greater full capacity level is a beneficial level scale effect.

When taking account of the potential benefits of these basic economies of scale it is essential to remember that there are no absolutes. In every case a limit is set by the availability of market opportunities. It is often claimed that serious errors of judgement were made in Britain in the choice of steel plant sizes in the 1960s, when too much emphasis was put on the size of Japanese plant and too little attention was paid to the different sizes of the markets which they supplied.

Another relevant lesson on 'real' economies of scale was learned in the same decade by oil companies marketing imported finished products in Third World countries. Some governments decided that they would prefer to import crude oil rather than finished products, and to have value added in local refinery operations. The initial reaction of oil companies was that such operations would be uneconomical because of the small sizes of the local markets. At the time capacities in excess of about 1 million tonnes per annum were considered necessary in order to be economical: anything less would suffer from diseconomies of scale. In the event refineries for Third World markets were designed and constructed with capacities well below that level. To the surprise of many people in the industry, careful design and construction, combined with a lean operation, produced remarkably efficient and economical plants.

The Philips Electronics Company had a somewhat similar experience when they embarked on the fundamental design of factory production methods for Third World locations. Instead of simply constructing a small-scale version of a European factory, they rewrote the design brief to reflect the different environment. One item in the brief was the minimization of the capital investment. This caused fundamental redesign of some processes. The lesson to be learned from the experiences of these oil and electronics industries is the same – that sometimes we have unwittingly incorporated what a colleague of mine described as 'gold plated technologies'; these have distorted true economies of scale, leading us to believe that we need to be bigger than is really necessary. There was good reason for Henry Ford and Charles Kettering (of General Motors) to be constantly repeating 'Build simplicity into it!' Some years ago Dr Ernst Fuhrmann, President of Porsche, said 'If I were a big company I would tell my engineers to design a very primitive car that could be repaired with five or ten tools. It would not be a bad car – but it would be a reliable one; and I think people would buy it. Complications are a source of additional defects.'

## Scale and Administration

One of the commonest claims for economies of scale is the benefit of shared overheads. Surely the work can be done more efficiently and at less cost in a single amalgamated organization, than in several independent small groups! In reality there is little evidence to justify a claim for cost or operational effectiveness. On the contrary, such are the natural tendencies for 'empire building' that the large centralized administration can easily become remote and therefore ineffective; it can also become introspective and self-justifying. Functional pressures can be very strong, making it difficult for top management to resist amalgamations. Such cost reductions as may be genuine are usually marginal. They are mostly not comparable to the damage that can be done by removing control from a general manager. Unfortunately, that damage cannot be quantified before the event, whereas anticipated cost savings easily can be. My own refusal on one occasion to accept proposals for amalgamations of administrative functions because of a conviction that a general manager must be held fully accountable was completely justified by results. Without that total accountability I am certain that major improvements in all the operations would not have been achieved. The danger is that decisions can too often be influenced by quantifiable factors, and insufficient weight given to qualitative matters that require judgement.

> For his different purposes man needs many different structures, both small ones and large ones, some exclusive and some comprehensive. For every activity there is a certain appropriate scale.
>
> E. F. Schumacher[2]

Remorselessly, as shop-floor, direct unit labour costs have been reduced, so that they frequently amount to no more than between five and fifteen per cent of the total manufacturing costs in engineering plants, the proportion absorbed in overheads has grown considerably. With the cost of bought-in materials and services being typically about half the total cost – and sometimes as much as 70 per cent – overheads are often appreciably more than the costs of direct production manpower. Obviously overhead costs are properly a matter of concern. Unfortunately, more often than not, they are a result of scrupulously tracking the small percentage of direct labour costs. This may be little more than an accident of history: there was a time when business was simpler and direct labour costs were seen as the main variable cost. Looking for overhead economies through amalgamation in order to obtain economies of scale is a will-o'-the-wisp. It merely diverts attention from the real economy potential in materials purchasing. The overhead concerned with direct labour costs should be no greater than can be justified by the magnitude of those costs and the influence that administration can have on them.

## Size and Purchasing

Every retailer recognizes the critical role of purchasing for business success, and buyers are among the most highly paid and valued employees. In many manufacturing companies purchasing personnel do not enjoy such high ranking in the company hierarchy. In one company I investigated critical decisions were being taken by a comparatively junior clerk, who was fairly well experienced but there was little interest from any member of the management. In that case material purchases accounted for nearly 70 per cent of total company operating costs. Attacking material costs is certainly not a glamorous task, and it can be difficult when a change of supplier or the use of an alternative material upsets product designers and production engineers. However, focusing attention on this crucial element of costs can produce amazing results.

One of the outstanding features of the past two or three decades has been an increase in the availability of a much wider range of materials. The changes that will challenge managements in the future will undoubtedly in many cases involve changes in material. The range to choose from is likely to increase at an even faster rate.

Materials purchasing is as much a professional job in manufacturing as it is in retailing. It interacts with all parts of the manufacturing organization and consequently it not only needs to have appropriate status, but also to have the interest and support of senior management if interdepartmental conflicts of interest are to be creative. I know from personal experience that such involvement can pay handsomely, particularly in medium- or large-scale enterprises where the difficulties of resolving conflicts tend to grow as the size and complexity of organization increases.

The volume size of purchases is another matter of concern for both big and small companies. In the absence of legislation prohibiting price discrimination, big customers are able, by means of the exercise of 'purchasing muscle', to obtain very big discounts far in excess of the supplier's savings resulting from the 'real' economies of scale. These seldom amount to more than about five per cent of the price. (In the United States the Robinson–Patman Act was passed in order to obviate excessive abuse of 'purchasing muscle'.) If a major

> I and others are devoted to the idea of obtaining simultaneously the
> massive resources of the large together with the speed of movement,
> closeness to the market and greater personal satisfaction of the small.
> Nevertheless the onus of proof is in my view on demonstrating that the
> large is able to do things that the small cannot, as well as not
> hampering the smaller units. The necessity therefore to ensure that
> size does not become an aim in itself is overriding.
>
> *John Harvey-Jones*[3]

company producing a five per cent net profit on turnover can obtain,
for example, a 20 per cent average discount on all materials
purchases, with total materials costs accounting for 50% of the sales
turnover, the discounts represent twice the net profit earned. If such a
company was limited to a maximum discount of five per cent it would
trade at a loss. The existence of inflated 'purchasing muscle'
discounts greatly distorts the true financial efficiency of a company,
but a more serious consequence is that suppliers necessarily have to
arrange their pricing structures to allow for high volume discounts:
this inevitably means that small companies buying small volumes are
effectively subsidizing big companies, and masking the comparative
operational inefficiency of the bigger company with its costly
overhead. This is probably the biggest distortion preventing a
true comparison of operational efficiency based directly on published
company accounts. If, in future, we are to achieve a mixture of
company and unit sizes that is optimal in terms of 'real' efficiency of
operation, effective legislative limits on volume discounts will have to
be introduced wherever it does not already exist.

## Size and Pricing

I believe that in much of the European market there has been a drift
towards unnecessary oligopoly and a blunting of real competition.
Domination of the retail trade by a small number of multiple stores
and supermarkets has both greatly reduced the scope for serious price
competition and decreased to a considerable extent the opportunities
of small manufacturers to find High Street outlets. Another
consequence is that many major suppliers have their margins
seriously squeezed because of the purchasing power of the retailers.

It is claimed that economies of scale create an imperative towards this concentration of business in comparatively few very big retail companies. If this claim were true one would expect to see prices paid by customers decreasing progressively in real terms with the passage of time. In some cases, such as with domestic appliances, this has happened. However, closer inspection shows that the lower cost is not a result of economies of scale in bigger company operations, but is a consequence of advances in product and production technologies for a rapidly growing market. For many other products, such as bread and beer, the concentration of manufacture and marketing into a few giant companies has, despite advances in some technology, produced either no reduction or an increase in the real price paid by the customer.

A loaf of bread provides a useful illustration. In 1900 the price per pound to a British household was six-tenths of a penny. Allowing for sterling devaluation over the next eighty years that price would be 21p in 1980. In fact, average prices that year were in the range 25–28p in the shops. Few customers who have lived long enough to make a personal judgement would argue that the increased real price can be justified by improved quality.

The goods that are now cheaper and better because of technological developments unfortunately represent a small proportion of annual household expenditure; and this proportion will reduce further as they become more durable. Consumables on the other hand account for a considerable proportion of household expenditure. The large-scale modern system of production and marketing is highly intensive in energy, material and capital compared with the localized systems that were traditional in the early part of this century. In addition to the half a tonne of refuse created annually, on average, by every European household, a substantial proportion of the pollution and waste caused by agriculture, industry and commerce is either directly or indirectly associated with food, drink and other consumables. The strictly limited tolerance of the environment will not permit the continuation and expansion of the massive, complex, wasteful and polluting systems that we have created to carry out simple tasks that not many generations ago were largely carried out in the home. Independent researchers, such as Graham Bannock, have been unable to find genuine justification for the belief that concentration into a few giant organizations in itself produces economies of scale that we could not afford to lose. I have found myself in agreement, based on personal experience, with those observers who conclude that the principal motivation for economic concentration in western societies is to provide power, influence and security for managers in general but senior managers in particular.

## Size and Technology

Whilst the size, and size alone, of companies may not yield economies, is there not a danger that without them technological development would wither? Much of the latest justification for 'Europeanization' of business is that further concentration is needed if we are to compete with the advanced technologies of Japan and the US. Faced with an uncertain future, and a certain need for greater innovation, this is a question that must be taken seriously.

First we can consider traditional products and industries. For them most of the R&D has been directed by big companies for the purpose of enabling them to grow into giant companies. Not surprisingly they have seldom been producing technologies that would be particularly well suited to small-scale operations. On the other hand, many of the most modern technological developments, particularly in the field of microelectronics, have made possible the very efficient operation, on a small scale, of processes which previously were restricted to big volume production. Consequently many small plants are receiving a new lease of life through new technological economies. For many traditional products and industries there no longer seems to be a technological imperative requiring larger-scale operations and mergers on an international basis. Even in industries concerned with the production of basic materials, like steel, there is a growth of very efficient small manufacturing plants.

In the new, non-traditional industries the claim of a need for further concentration on grounds of technology is not entirely clear. The record of technologically led innovation is strongly on the side of small operators all over the world. Silicon Valley, in California and elsewhere, is a good illustration. In Japan Masar Ulbuka and Akio Morita started the Sony Company with 12 workers and £124 of capital. Of course it is often true that the conversion of a product and process development into production can be a costly and risky business. It is equally true that a major company may have a greater financial potential for financing a new venture. On the other hand, as someone who has been responsible for new product launches in a giant company, I know that there are many non-financial problems to be overcome, which outweigh the apparent financial advantages that hardly exist in small firms. A study made by the US National Science Foundation found that for every expenditure on innovation, small firms produce four times as much as medium-sized firms and twenty-four times as much as big firms. Of course I am not arguing that all innovation can come from small companies, but I do not believe that, because of some imagined technological imperative, further concentration of industrial and commercial enterprise is the key to general commercial competitiveness. Whatever may have been the minimum competitive sizes of particular activities in the past, modern technologies are moving the limit to even lower levels.

## Size and Marketing

Another spurious justification for large-scale operations is that by marketing internationally on a gigantic scale there is a reduction in the unit cost of elements of marketing because expenditure is very widely spread over a huge number of items. This by no means applies to all elements of marketing cost, and one of the biggest, which is distribution, is usually increased because items have to be carried over greater distances. One only has to imagine the difference between a loaf baked in a big, central factory and one produced in a local bakehouse to appreciate the difference. Furthermore, as Schumacher pointed out, there is absurd waste created by transporting biscuits baked in the south of England to Scotland for sale, and transporting other biscuits baked in Scotland to the south of England.[5] This surely is the kind of waste that is unacceptable as we strive to stabilize atmospheric carbon dioxide in the atmosphere. It is an irrational and unnecessary waste of real resources and a contribution to environmental damage.

> What is the meaning of democracy, freedom, human dignity, standard of living, self realisation, fulfilment? Is it a matter of goods or of people? Of course it is a matter of people. But people can be themselves only in small comprehensible groups. Therefore we must learn to think in terms of articulated structures that can cope with a multiplicity of small-scale units.
>
> *E. F. Schumacher*[4]

In reality the very concept of modern marketing is a product of the drive towards concentration of industrial and commercial activity. To a considerable extent it was evolved to give some appearance of competition once oligopoly had largely reduced the scope for product differentiation or price competition. It is absurd to refer to economies of scale in an activity much of which is irrelevant in small-scale local operations.

Undoubtedly there have developed some very considerable costs in the marketing of national or international brands that are inescapable for most big, mature companies that have grown up with them. I discovered, for example, how serious would be the consequences of unilaterally selling lubricating oil in a dispensing device – as it used to be – rather than in 'fruit' cans. One company with which I was associated inadvisedly stopped advertising a principal product, but quickly reinstated it when sales plunged. There would have been no such problem had all its competitors stopped advertising. For ordinary, everyday purchases advertising is not directed to increase total consumption: it aims to attract customers to a particular brand. You would not use less washing-up detergent if advertising by all brand-makers stopped. To a considerable extent advertising in big brand companies is a substitute for the reputation for good service which small companies can acquire, but which is so difficult for a much more remote and impersonal product source. The concept of the supermarket has been a godsend to big retailers and national brand producers. They no longer have to pretend to offer a good customer service – though they would obviously deny it; packaging and advertising are all they need now that customers serve themselves and deliver their own goods.

## Size and Profitability

Since it is proving so hard to find any real justification for the general claim to operate on an ever increasing scale with greater concentration in a few giant companies, can it be that the motivation for expansion, diversification, mergers and conglomerates is the attraction of greater profitability? Even if no benefits accrued to customers as a result, would equity shareholders benefit? Unfortunately there is no clear evidence from published information that most shareholders in major companies benefit from a steadily increasing return on their investment above that they might have gained from investments in smaller firms.

An examination of comparative earnings per US dollar of assets data[6] shows a striking difference between earnings per dollar of assets of small, medium, large and very large companies in five different types of business – manufacturing, services, construction, transport and wholesale/retail. In each sector the earnings were easily the highest in small firms with assets of $25,000 or less. As the size increased earnings fell until in the biggest group, with assets in excess of $100 m, earnings per dollar were half, or less, those of companies with assets between $0.5 m and $1 m.

There are various reasons why the differences may not be so great in Europe. If, however, the reverse were to be the case it could not be that the business environment in Europe is less favourable to big business than it is in the USA, where the market is more strongly regulated with anti-trust laws, and other legislation such as the Robinson–Patman Act.

Once again, it would not appear that there is any intrinsic reason why company size of itself should offer shareholders better return prospects. There is, nevertheless, a very clear general relationship – with some notable exceptions – between the emoluments of top managers, and others in senior positions, and the size of their companies.

## Small Firms Revival

As we face the radical changes and uncertainties of the New Age of business it is more important than ever for managers at all levels to face realities. Faith in falsehoods and illusions could prove disastrous. I happened to grow up in the environment of a small, family, retail business before spending nearly thirty years with one of the biggest

> As soon as great size has been created there is often a strenuous attempt to attain smallness with bigness. There is tremendous longing and striving to profit, if at all possible, from the convience, humanity and manageability of smallness.
>
> *E. F. Schumacher*[7]

companies in the world. As a result of those experiences, and of all that I have learned since whilst working to promote small businesses, I am in no doubt about the exaggerated claims for economies of scale, nor about blindness to their diseconomies. Furthermore, there are many differences between small and big firms, other than scale of operation, that managers should be aware of when seeking the optimum size for their particular operations. For it is no more true to say, as a generalization, that smallness is most efficient or desirable than it is to claim the same for bigness. For a variety of different reasons there are ideal sizes for different kinds of operation, because different purposes require different structures – some small, some medium and some big; some local and some widespread. We no more need an idolatory of smallness than we need the present idolatory of gigantism. If we are to remain healthy we have to discover the most appropriate size of operation for each particular business.

As a result of a deliberate post-war policy, Japan has always maintained a high proportion of employment in small firms. By 1970, in the USA, West Germany, France and Britain the proportion employed in firms of less than 100 had fallen to below 30 per cent – in Britain it was down to 17 per cent. Fortunately in the last twenty years there has been a significant reversal of the decline in most industrial countries. In Britain, for example, there was an increase of 60 per cent between 1970 and 1980.

This revival of small business in the industrialized countries is of great significance for Third World development, where labour is plentiful and capital scarce. Schumacher's concept of appropriate

---

Larger cities are by definition centralised, man-made environments that depend mainly on food, water, energy and other goods from outside. Smaller cities, by contrast, can be the heart of a community-based development and provide services to the surrounding countryside. Given the importance of cities, special efforts and safeguards are needed to ensure that the resources they demand are produced sustainably and that urban dwellers participate in decisions affecting their lives. Residential areas are likely to be more habitable if they are governed as individual neighbourhoods with direct local participation. To the extent that energy and other needs can be met on a local basis, both the city and the surrounding area will be better off.

*WCED Public Hearing, Ottawa, May 1986*

technology is universally applicable, even though it was initially expressed in a Third World context. He recognized that technology must be adapted to suit the needs of each individual community, making allowance for cultural circumstances and customs, as well as for the state of educational, social and economic development. Four requirements were identified as providing a sound basis for development.

1 Workplaces have to be created in the places where people are living, thereby avoiding migration and excessive urbanization.
2 On average, a workplace must not require more capital than represented by two or three years' average earnings.
3 Production and other methods employed must match the skills and educational attainment potential of the local population.
4 Maximum possible use should be made of local or indigenous materials; products should be produced primarily for the needs of the local population.

An extremely important challenge to European industrial companies lies in the recognition that development of the virgin market potential of the Third World – where nearly 85 per cent of the world's population will be living by the year AD 2000 – depends upon the creation of 'added value' by that massive work-force with the minimum of capital investment in each workplace. Only by the internal development of purchasing power in each country does the potential transform into a real market. There is a great opportunity for European companies to transfer some of the 'appropriate productive technologies' that are necessary to enable Third World businessmen and women to accelerate the pace of that local grassroots development. However, the technologies must be tailored to the needs, means and circumstances of local communities.

## Towards a Better Balance – Horses for Courses

It would seem that most things in the real business world – technological developments, work pattern trends, environmental concerns, resource problems, social limits to growth, the striving for individualization of design and quality of product, the need to reduce some of the unnecessary stress of life and waste – point to a continuation of the trend to a better balanced mixture of large, medium-sized and small businesses, with a much bigger part for the small and medium sizes. Of course it is not a trend that suits everyone. Financial institutions in particular are much more comfortable dealing with large organizations and large sums of money. However, in recent years some of them have been reorganizing to provide better, tailor-made services for small business clients.

An ideology, and indeed a mythology, of growth has evolved in the past century as industry and commerce have moved from one stage to another. Technological imperative is one part of this mythology. It would be a disaster for everyone, not least for managers and companies, if they continued to submit to this idea. As an engineer and technologist I am convinced that we do not have to submit to whatever bigger and more complex technologies may be suggested as being most beneficial to financial interests. Technologies that are harmonious with the environment and are sustainable in terms of resources can be, and must be, made to serve the needs of people. The new directions of product and process development will have to be determined by managers and technologists; financial resources will have to be made to fulfil their fundamental purpose, which is to facilitate such development and not to determine its goal.

Of course, there will be enormous resistance to such radical changes. There is fear that any departure from the paths that we have followed would be disastrous for all, and that personal sacrifice and loss would be involved. But those fears stem largely from a genuine belief in the ideology of corporate growth. The first step towards a new direction for business development is to question doubtful assumptions with an open mind and to search for truth and reality. We are at the crossroads.

Happily there are people in high places that have been facing hard and sometimes painful conclusions. Siccolt Mansholt, one of the architects of the European Common Agricultural Policy, has said that the drive towards large-scale energy- and chemical-intensive agriculture has been a fundamental mistake, and a quite different and more environmentally harmonious form of farming needs to replace it. Sir Adrian Cadbury, when he was Chairman of the Cadbury Schweppes food and drink group wrote in *The Guardian*: 'We shall need to reverse the trend of the last twenty years towards large centralised organisations . . . Big is expensive and inflexible . . . We want to break these big organisations down into their separate business units and to give those companies freedom.' Unfortunately in the same article he also wrote that 'Large companies will become more like federations of small enterprises' without giving any reason why the small enterprises should not become entirely separate and free-standing entities. Perhaps this separation will in many instances follow by means of management and employee buy-outs once freedom has been experienced.

The more that managers can begin to think the unthinkable and contemplate reversing the trend, as Sir Adrian has done, the more likely we are to see the innovation needed in an age of fundamental change and uncertainty.

## Notes

* T. K. Quinn, *Giant Business: Threat to Democracy*. Exposition Press, New York, 1953.
1 D. Gabor, *Inventing the Future*. Pelican, 1964.
2 E. F. Schumacher, *Small is Beautiful*.
3 J. Harvey-Jones, *Making it Happen*.
4 E. F. Schumacher, *Small is Beautiful*.
5 Ibid.
6 Office of the Secretary of the US Treasury and Office of Tax, *Harvard Business Review*, January/February 1979.
7 E. F. Schumacher, *Small is Beautiful*.

# The Numbers Game

The most fruitful thing in the world is a valid new concept which by virtue of its truth can serve as a signpost for action.

E. F. Schumacher*

Manufacturing industry played a leading part in the phenomenon of corporate gigantism. It was in manufacturing that the substitution of capital investment in technology for employment of labour first went hand in hand with a growth of belief in the economies of scale. Each of the aspects of the anticipated benefits of size that were discussed in chapter 3 – administration, purchasing, pricing, technology, marketing and profitability – had a numerical evaluation system associated with it. If some of those anticipations have not been entirely justified, doubt must be cast on the validity of some of the concepts embodied in the evaluation systems. Furthermore, a change in the size distribution of companies that is required for sustainable development will need to be accompanied by a critical review of existing numerical systems, and then their replacement by alternatives that reflect the necessary conditions for sustainability.

This chapter is about the numbers that managers use in planning, implementation of plans, motivation of people, monitoring and evaluating performance. Numbers are the language of measurement. The ones that we use are those that describe the particular things that we choose to measure. They are never more than a few that have been selected from a wide range of possible measurements. The selection is obviously an extremely important decision, because it will have a most profound effect on all other decisions. Thus anything that influences our choice of measurements is of critical concern. Our values are the principal determinant of that choice. Since the paradigm change in which we are living involves value changes, such as were discussed in chapter 2, it is essential that the numbers that we use to measure our business should be altered to reflect those changes in values.

## Numbers with Real and Relevant Meaning

Numbers are mercurial things. They can enlighten; but they can also deceive. Not infrequently they do neither because they have no recognizable meaning. Unless numbers have relevant meaning – telling their own clear story – they may at best have no value for all practical purposes; at worst they can mislead. A most valuable by-product of business computer application is that it makes people think more carefully than ever before about the relevance and meaning of the numbers that they have been using, and about what they need to know and understand, precisely, in order to do their jobs. Numbers are essential for effective action. It is of little use to know that something is getting better or worse unless one knows by how much. Quantity gives weight and usefulness to qualitative information, but only as long as the qualitative message is clear.

I first learned to be cautious about numbers when I was a young research engineer. The number in question was the octane number of motor spirit. The simple definition of a fuel's octane number is the measure of its propensity to 'knock' in a spark ignition engine. It is expressed as having equal propensity to a percentage of a pure hydrocarbon – iso octane – in a mixture with another pure hydrocarbon – normal heptane. The difficulties start when samples of motor spirit are put in different engines and the tendency to 'knock' compared with that of mixtures of the two pure hydrocarbons. The sample appears to have different octane numbers in different engines. What possible use can it be if octane numbers are different in various, common car engines? It only gains real commercial meaning and usefulness when it expresses the proportion of cars that are free from 'knock' when the spirit is in normal road operation. So for quality control purposes we had to redefine the meaning of octane number so that the equivalence was not simply a comparison in a single engine, but in a total car population. There were two lessons for me in that experience. First, be careful not to accept conventional wisdom or definitions as the truth. Second, be observant: try to keep the whole system picture in mind. Things would have been very different in so many parts of engineering if we had paid attention to the whole system instead of concentrating on one aspect. For example, the traditional approach to power station development has been to obtain the greatest electricity output with the minimum consumption of fuel, and largely to ignore the use of energy remaining in the stack gases. As a result, about two-thirds of the energy content of the fuel is wasted because we have not considered the total system. We have only been concerned to generate electricity.

Towards the end of my business career, as a company chairman and chief executive, conversations with colleagues quite frequently revealed that the numbers that were our common currency had different meanings for some people, and no meaning at all for others. A management team cannot function effectively if members are reading different messages into the numbers they are given. It pays dividends to spend time and money gaining a common understanding.

This book is about managing uncertainty in a period of fundamental change. Hazel Henderson, a leading radical economist and thinker, makes a very relevant point for the present generation of managers: 'One of the key elements in all such transition periods and changing worldviews is the shift in perception of what is important, what is valuable, the goals to be pursued and the ways to measure collective progress towards these goals.'[1] We need to be clear that all the measurements that we use daily are the products of different times, some of which are very distant while others are more recent. They may or may not be very useful in years to come. This suggests that there is a need for a regular audit of measurements.

## Averages and Money Measurements

Averages comprise one category of measurements that will need to be watched even more carefully then hitherto. When conditions are reasonably stable, and change is continuous, they can be useful; and they are attractive because they simplify what may be very complex pictures. As change accelerates and becomes more fragmentary, traditional averages can quickly lose meaning and may even be misleading.

Measurements in terms of money are dominant in business numbers. Obviously money flows and stocks are a vital part of management concern. But money has a great power of attraction because it can be used as a measure of value. Consequently much information about non-monetary matters has been translated into money terms. Take, for example, sales statistics. Although it is articles and services that are sold, by the time the information reaches senior managers it will probably have been converted into money. This money-dominated style of management is a product of history, dating particularly from the era of 'scientific management', in which business was perceived as nothing more than a money-making machine. Naturally, with such a model, management became infiltrated by accountants, who liked everything to be expressed in terms of money. The transition that is in process demands attention to real values as well as to necessary money measurements. Individual managers must decide which particular real factors are important and valuable in relation to the particular goals that are being pursued. Only then can a useful decision be made about what must be measured to reveal progress. This is not as easy as it may sound. Managers are busy people and seldom have the necessary time for the careful and sometimes lengthy study that is required to make useful choices of parameters and measuring instruments. It is a demanding intellectual task, and it is important that managers be given the necessary professional assistance for the task.

There was a time when money values were comparatively stable. A feature of the closing decades of the twentieth century is the volatility of money. This makes it a very elastic measure, and that is not the most desirable characteristic of a measuring instrument. Money is a vital element and factor of production, which, when combined with human talent, its products – machines, and natural resources, produces a business. In future it will be just as important, if not more so, to pay keen attention to the money element in business, but other non-money elements will have to be given much more attention than hitherto, and it will not help if they are disguised by a translation into money language.

## Whither DCF?

Discounted cash flow (DCF) is an example of a project evaluation technique, based on the principle of compound interest, which over a period gained favour in many companies as a replacement for 'accountancy rate of return'. It was commended for a variety of good reasons. It promised to minimize uncertainty, describing reality more closely, by looking at the whole expected life of the project in the real world. In particular it recognized that a dollar or mark or franc or pound in hand today is more valuable than one at some future date. Furthermore it avoided distortions present in previous methods of project evaluation, such as the assumption that depreciation of a physical asset occurs as an annual cost.

DCF served us well as long as we did not need to be concerned about such things as externality costs, environmental degradation and depletion of increasingly scarce natural resources. No longer is sustainable economic development seen as a hobby-horse of a school of academic economists. It is the claimed intention of most European governments. This means that European businesses are being required to operate under the restraint of what is sustainable in the use of resources and the environment. As I discovered myself when I was responsible for oil product changes that had an environmental benefit – such as introducing lead-free fuel – it was not commercially possible to act unilaterally in some markets in the absence of a restraining framework. It has taken more than twenty years in Europe for government agreements to be reached so that all may use such a product in their cars. Problems such as the greenhouse effect require restraint now, not in twenty years time. Common international constraining legislation will be required, but it will take time. Meanwhile, because it is in the interests of all, including businesses, that sustainable measures should be introduced urgently, industrial and commercial associations will need to get together and evolve guidelines and codes of practice – such as they have for safety and toxicity – that will take account of resource and environmental concerns, as well as the purely financial attractiveness of particular proposals.

Major investment decisions are not usually taken on the basis of a single proposed solution. Alternatives are available from which a choice is made. It will be in the comparison of one scheme with another that the information dealing with real resources and environmental consequences can have an influence on decisions. New evaluation techniques will need to be developed to ensure sustainable prosperity in the long term as well as short- and medium-term financial attraction. These techiques will, in essence, prevent indiscriminate discounting of long-term adverse consequences. The danger of using DCF alone in its present form is that a benefit or cost that occurs late in the life of a project has little influence on the decision to proceed or not.

## Manufacturing versus Reconditioning

In 1977 I commissioned a study to define the most attractive way of at least doubling the average life of cars. With the passage of time the average life had been gradually declining in Britain until, at the time the study was undertaken, it was only a little more than ten years. The main conclusion of the study was that a reconditioning operation on existing designs was in various ways preferable to a new design that would be intrinsically more durable. This conclusion seemed, at first sight, to be at variance with the common notion that factory production is more productive and efficient than garage repair or reconditioning operations. It was encouraging to learn that a study made concurrently by the Batelle Research Centre in Geneva, commissioned by the EEC in Brussels, showed that in France not only could reconditioning almost halve consumption of materials and energy used in the car manufacturing industry, but there would be a worthwhile reduction in expense incurred by motorists and a substantial net increase in overall employment.

These two studies called into question the belief that labour-intensive/low-capital 'garage-type' operations are poor at adding value compared with factory production. That belief appears to be well founded and confirmed by the almost negligible effect that expenditure on garage services has in most cases on the second-hand market value of cars. The false signal arises from the fact that there is no valid relationship between second-hand market value and the intrinsic value of the vehicle as a provider of transportation.

Before those two studies were made I had, like most other people, assumed that factories produced things, and that productivity and efficiency needed to be measured in terms of the quantity of resources used in the production of a single unit thing. What I overlooked was that in the case of a car the real product is a period of transportation. Similarly for all other hardware products, the real output is a period of useful service that the thing will provide. Consequently, when considering productivity and efficiency of factory operations, the measure should be the quantity of resources used per month or year of useful average service that the product has been designed to provide. We should not, as has been traditional, disregard the time factor, as though factories were creating products with an everlasting life. Some of the apparently improved productivity in certain industries has been achieved at the cost of reduced durability of products.

When we change the method of measuring efficiency and productivity to 'resource cost per unit of useful average service life' we immediately have the possibility of a direct comparison between factory and repair/reconditioning operations. Both are seen to be producing the same output – so much useful service time. A domestic washing machine may provide an illustration. The factory gate cost may be £250 for a machine with an average seven-year life. The cost of a thorough reconditioning job that could extend its useful life by a similar amount should not exceed £200. Consequently the cost per annum of useful life added by reconditioning is somewhat less than £30, whereas the factory cost is about £36. It may be possible to design a much more durable machine for which the cost per average useful year of service is less than £30. However, even in that case, the reconditioning cost may be even lower because the reconditioning takes place with more durable replacement components on a machine which is intrinsically more durable.

> The concept of 'cost' is essentially different as between renewable and non-renewable goods, as also between manufactures and services. In fact it can be said that economics, as currently constituted fully applies only to manufactures, but is being applied without discrimination to all goods and services, because an appreciation of the essential, qualitative differences between the four categories is lacking.
>
> *E. F. Schumacher*[2]

It would be wrong to think that repair/reconditioning operations of all hardware products are more cost-effective than the manufacturing operation. The lower the factory gate cost of an article the less likely is that to be so. However, for a very wide range of manufactured products it is important to understand that large reductions in material and energy consumption, which will be priority objectives of the New Age, may be obtained, without a loss of real productivity or resource efficiency, by the introduction of reconditioning as a standard practice. The use of the proposed method of measurement, introducing the average useful period of service, will enable realistic decisions to be made.

# The Balance between Money and Manpower

The idea that productivity is best measured by the amount of added value created by each employee has its origin in the age of hand tools and primitive machine tools, when the speed of production was determined by the operator. Despite the fact that the speed of most modern production is a function of the technologies used rather than of the numbers of people employed, the most common measure of productivity remains output per employee.

Managers obviously need to be in control of manpower costs. The ratio output per employee has no useful absolute meaning in that complex task, but it is a useful indicator of trends. On its own, it has no clear significance as a measure of productivity. A clear picture of productivity can only be obtained if all the inputs to the business operation are related to the output. Effective management requires that each element of input needs to be monitored separately in relation to the level of business, with comparisons made both to the targeted quantity and the historic trend. This may sound like a very trite remark. However, many businesses that are increasingly capital intensive show a productivity of investment which is either not improving or declining, and this calls into question the detail of the monitoring of productivity in common practice.

From what has just been said there is no single measure of productivity that can take the place of the separate elements measurements. However, I have found one relationship that is useful in making comparisons between companies: I believe it is not in common use and can be helpful in a consideration of the most appropriate balance between investment and manpower in a particular situation. It is especially illuminating when the relationships are shown diagrammatically.

## Financial Productivity

All businesses are concerned with adding value. The smaller the total resource inputs required in producing a unit of added value, the more financially productive the company is. There are just two financial inputs that are combined in the process of adding value: manpower costs and total capital employed. In figure 4.1 the financial performance can be represented, for a particular year, by a single

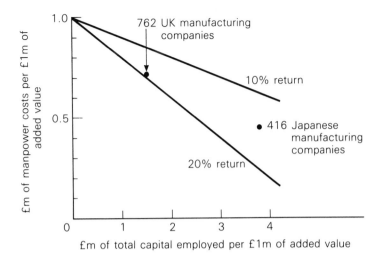

Figure 4.1 A comparison of different balances between manpower and investment as they affect financial productivity.

point. I first came upon this form of representation when playing with some numbers quoted by Dr F. E. Jones FRS.[3] Comparative figures were given for British Leyland Motor Company and Toyota of Japan; the British Steel Corporation and New Nippon Steel of Japan; and 416 Japanese and 762 UK manufacturing companies. They covered the following parameters – total numbers of employees, total capital investment, total sales revenue, total bought-in materials, goods and services. By subtracting the total purchases from sales revenue, added value was obtained.

In order to obtain a common basis for comparison of manpower and investment inputs it seemed reasonable to use £1m of added value as the output factor. Coincidentally, the average annual cost per employee for the 762 UK manufacturing companies and the 416 Japanese companies was the same, at £3,500, in the years chosen for comparison. The lines marked 10% return and 20% return on figure 4.1 are such that any point on them represents the same rate of return with different combinations of manpower and capital. Thus, if a return of 10 per cent on total capital employed was required to show a satisfactory financial performance, there was no great difference at that time between the Japanese and UK manufacturing companies, though the British had a slight advantage with their higher manpower

**Table 4.1**   Manpower and money in UK and Japanese manufacturing companies

| Per £1m of added value per annum | UK | Japan |
|---|---|---|
| Number of employees | 204 | 130 |
| Cost per annum of each employee | £3,500 | £3,500 |
| Total capital employed | £1.5m | £3.8m |

level and lower capital investment. Furthermore, if – as in the UK – a higher return than 10 per cent was required, the Japanese mixture of manpower and capital was much less attractive than the UK one. Although at the time the British combination was incapable of producing the higher return required in the high money-cost environment, an attempt to move all UK manufacturing firms to a Japanese-type combination would have made things worse. The Japanese high capital/low labour combination was well suited to the very low money-cost environment that their manufacturing businesses enjoy.

Analysis based on 'unit added value' as the denominator is invaluable, for the simple reason that, in purely financial terms, added value is the true financial output of a product, plant or business. Had managements used it more many important lessons would have been learned. For example, some companies would have realized that their product mixture contained too high a proportion of low added value items. One of Shell's great strengths during my time in the company was that we had an added value product mixture that was above average. In some industries it can take almost as much investment and manpower to produce low added value products as it does to produce products of a higher value.

## A Range of Manpower/Investment Inputs can be Equally Productive

However, the main point that I wish to make is that this type of analysis will, I believe, become even more important in years of increasing uncertainty. The comparison in figure 4.1 of a wide selection of Japanese and UK manufacturing firms shows that, at the same level of unit manpower cost, similar returns on investment can be made with widely different mixtures of manpower and investment. This conclusion from averages of large numbers of companies cannot, of course, be said to apply to every single business in the two groups. Each point represents a wide range of mixtures in its component members. However, separate analyses of a number of different industries show that in most there is a range of combinations that are capable of producing comparable manpower remuneration and return on investment. It appears to be incorrect to suggest that a higher manpower/lower investment mixture will inevitably require lower pay or lower returns or both.

Therefore, if we start by a consideration of several alternative combinations of manpower and investment, each of which gives comparable prospects of pay and return on investment per 'unit of added value', an important choice becomes available. Whenever there is a time of great uncertainty, aiming for a high capital investment solution is obviously a greater business risk; a low-capital solution of comparable financial productivity is more prudent. Many companies have followed that principle in the past when investing in countries in which political stability has been uncertain. The uncertainties that will be faced in future (even in countries that *are* politically stable) whilst they are different in character, nevertheless present just as great risks. In most large companies there is a considerable tendency to prefer the employment of money rather than of people. If unnecessary risks are to be avoided in the face of uncertainty this tendency needs to be strongly resisted.

## Matching Production with a Market

The choice of an appropriate balance between capital and labour is one that can only be made in the context of a defined size of market and market share. A company may have domestic outlets for its products over a wide geographical area that could be supplied from a single production centre. Alternatively it may have a choice in supplying its customers from several, strategically distributed production centres. Depending upon the choice made as to the most satisfactory way of planning its production, so the capital/labour mixture is likely to differ from one that would have better suited a different production option. In order to obtain the best possible business organization it is essential that the choice of the production capital/labour mixture should be made at the same time as the decisions about the most appropriate to match production with the market. There will usually be a tendency to choose the option involving the minimum number of production sites. In some instances this may produce the best results; but I have known cases where several sites with a different capital/labour combination were preferable to a single, highly capital-intensive site. It is prudent not to assume that a single site will inevitably be the best choice.

## GNP: Grossly-misleading National Product?

For many years consumption of most commodities and goods maintained a fairly steady relationship with changes in overall economic activity as expressed by GNP or GDP. In the case of the energy industries, for example, a 1 per cent increase in GNP resulted in approximately the same percentage increase in energy consumption. This historic relationship changed as a result of disturbances caused by the fourfold increase in oil prices in 1974 and the energy conservation practices that were subsequently introduced. Ten years later some industrialized countries were increasing their GNP with little or no change in energy consumption. Thus the relationship of 1 per cent to 1 per cent, which was so useful and convenient for planning departments, has been lost. Many more relationships are likely to be upset as economic development moves from what might be described as indiscriminate consumption to a more discriminating and conserving approach. Those concerned with the development of company plans based to some extent on a perception of the general change in the state of the economy will need to be cautious about the use of historically based ratios.

It is sometimes forgotten by business people that GNP only measures one particular part of economic life. It is no more and no less than the sum of all activities that involve a financial transaction. It excludes all those human activities, which are often the same as those involved in financial transactions, that do not involve an exchange of money. For example, cooking a meal at home and buying the same meal in a restaurant differ, from a GNP perception, the former being excluded, the latter included. Indeed a significant part

---

It will not be easy to learn economic wisdom. But if we do not the human race may well be numbered amongst the species that have become extinct.

*E. F. Schumacher*[1]

of GNP growth this century has been the transfer of activities from either the domestic or charitable sectors, which were previously not counted, to the sector of traded goods and services. The growth of DIY has begun to reverse that change, taking some economic activity out of measured GNP performance. As more leisure time becomes available and it becomes easier, with new technologies, to carry out tasks domestically that previously have been part of the measured economy, GNP change will increasingly provide false signals to businesses that supply the domestic and gift economies.

The paradigm shift that is occurring is the result of a variety of fundamental changes – human perceptions and attitudes, the nature and arrangements of work, social and physical limits to growth, environmental and resource problems that are becoming dominant considerations in development. Each one of these factors creates a new problem and a new challenge to managements: they must choose numbers that they will need to use if they are to succeed in the innovatory entrepreneurial task that is demanded of them. The old measurements belong to a simpler age. There will be many more dials to watch in years to come, and managers will need considerable assistance from business statisticians and analysts in the development and choice of appropriate, new indicators. The business 'numbers game' is becoming more and more complicated.

## Summary

Every management is using a variety of numerical measurements to help plan, monitor and control its business. Most of these measurements have evolved gradually over many decades to reflect what was at the time considered to be an improvement in judging the performance, actual or potential, of some particular aspect of the business. For example, 'Discounted Cash Flow' came to be preferred to 'pay-out period' as a method of judging the attractiveness of an investment. That particular choice, like all other choices of parameters, reflected the contemporary assumptions and beliefs of economic life. As was discussed in chapter 1, those assumptions and beliefs were flawed or mistaken ideas about the real planetary economy. No matter what fine words may be spoken or written in a company's strategy statements, so long as the old criteria are used the direction in which the business is moving will not change. Each of the numbers in common use in a company must be critically examined to discover in what ways, and to what extent, the underlying assumptions and beliefs that are embodied in its meaning are at variance with the new vision and values that have been chosen for the company. Where the old numbers are producing misleading signals they must be replaced by new ones that are true to the new intention and understanding.

## Notes

\* G. Kirk, ed., *Schumacher on Energy*. Abacus, London, 1983, p. 153.
1 H. Henderson, speech at The Other Economic Summit, London, 1985.
2 E. F. Schumacher, *Small is Beautiful*.
3 F.E. Jones, The Economic Ingredients of Industrial Success. The James Clayton Lecture to the Institution of Mechanical Engineers, 1976.
4 E. F. Schumacher, *Small is Beautiful*.

# 5

# Good Work – Different Arrangements

People can be themselves only in small comprehensible groups.
Therefore we must learn to think in terms of an articulated structure
that can cope with a multiplicity of small-scale units.

E. F. Schumacher*

Some of the most commonly used parameters in business management
are ratios which have numbers of employees as the denominator.
Each one is supposed to indicate a level of labour productivity in a
particular area. Such ratios were introduced when the whole of a
certain activity was carried out entirely by company employees. Now
that work is often arranged differently, many of the ratios no longer
serve a useful purpose and may be misleading. For example, when
some of the activities of a department are being taken over by a
service company, a false picture of departmental productivity will be
obtained if the number of employees in the department is used as the
denominator in a productivity ratio.

Among the several major changes that are having an increasing
influence on the way in which work is organized and carried out, are a
range of ideas about what constitutes 'good work': they correspond
with the needs, expectations and attitudes of people and companies.
By examining how changing ideas about work, jobs, employment and
self-employment relate to the needs of a business in the future, we
may be able to glimpse something of the variety of different ways that
work *can* be organized, and the different qualities of leadership that
managers will have to develop.

The deep pyramid structures, with their complex bureaucracies,
the micro-division of labour and the concentration of workpeople
into plants and offices housing thousands, have slowly evolved over
the past two centuries. Before the emergence of the big textile mills,

coal-mines and steelworks, labour had been organized in gangs. In the absence of cheap and rapid means of communication and transport, factories were necessarily located close to sources of power and water. Employees had to be housed nearby, and the multiplicity of services required by both the factories and the population grew up around them. In Europe during the nineteenth century there was a vast migration from the villages and small country towns into the great industrial and commercial centres. Urbanization and industrialization went hand in hand, and were interdependent. This process of the concentration of population has continued in advanced industrial countries until very recently. However, within the past few decades a reverse process of population dispersal has begun.

There were two phases in industrial concentration. Initially workers were gathered into factories to man machines that performed a particular process of manufacture, such as spinning. The second phase began when the various processes involved in the production of a finished product were amalgamated in a single plant. The most extreme example of this form of integration came with Henry Ford's automobile plants in Detroit, in which iron ore and coal entered at one end and a finished car rolled off the production line at the other. As organizations grew, more and more people were required to administer increasingly complex operations, and the tasks of management became more like the command of armies. Not surprisingly industry and commerce evolved comparable military-style hierarchical and bureaucratically disciplined structures.

The influences that were at work in this historical, evolutionary process are no longer so widespread nor so strong. For example, cheap and easy means of transport and communication are now widely available in the developed countries. There is no longer the need to employ the whole work-force on a single site. Many of the functions, particularly those handling information, can be dispersed; and even the Ford Motor Company no longer pursues the total integration of production. As some of the pressures that helped to produce concentration into massive organizations begin to decrease, there are other new influences that are the motive forces in the reorganization of work in factories, offices, shops and many other institutions. Three of the most important new factors are new technology, new attitudes and new expectations.

## The Influence of New Technology on Work

New technology is having, and will increasingly continue to have, as profound an influence on the way that work is organized, and on work people, as traditional technology had throughout the industrial age. Its effects promise to be very different from the old technology – in some ways quite the opposite. This must inevitably dramatically change the nature of business management, most of all its human aspects.

Until quite recently automatic machines converted skilled, manual machine operators into deskilled, automatic machine minders. As automation displaces much of the deskilled routine work of production, the role of people directly involved changes. Although fewer in number – even in the assembly shops – skill requirements become much greater in the design, control, supervision and adjustment of very sophisticated and highly integrated systems composed of electronically controlled electromechanical units. The industrial plant operator becomes more like an airline pilot, mainly identifying and dealing skilfully with disturbances by taking appropriate corrective action, rather than performing a simple repetitive routine. Exceptionally there must be the capability of handling a major breakdown in the system, bringing the expensive plant, as it were, to a safe landing. It is sometimes claimed that a mass production factory worker could be trained for a particular task in a matter of two or three hours; the New Age front-line plant operatives require not only considerable skill training and they also need to have a substantial understanding of complex systems and the ability to make rapid individual judgements.

Under the old regime the design of factory organization was primarily machine-orientated. The human factor in its many micro-divisions filled the gaps between machines. In the New Era effective utilization of high capital plant can only be obtained if the system is carefully designed to match human skills and characteristics with plant requirements. Computer integrated maufacturing (CIM) demands a fundamental reassessment by managements – to be 'people led' rather than 'technology led'.

## Computer Integrated Manufacturing

Some companies are paying a high price because they have not understood this simple yet profound fact. Studies by management consultants A. T. Kearney and the Ingersoll Group into the effects of major investments in computer integrated manufacturing technology clearly show that, where there has been failure to achieve improvements, in such things as deadlines for completion of orders, stock control and quality of production, there has been no reorientation and involvement of employees. Company managements have mistakenly believed that the new investment would of itself produce the desired results. They failed to see that the crucial element, the key to success, exists at the interface between human and machine systems. In such firms the result is that systems are taking much longer to install; they then suffer from excessive breakdown and the new 'flexible manufacturing' proves to be less flexible than the traditional disintegrated systems.

The crucial importance of the interface between human and machine systems became apparent when we first began to explore the prospects of 'total oil refinery automation' in the 1960s. It is an enlightening experience that many others have had, particularly in process industries and in others like the design of aircraft cockpit control systems. No doubt the lesson has been more difficult to learn in the more labour-intensive production line factories in which Taylorism and Fordism divided work progressively over many years into thousands of smaller and smaller repetitive units. Having fragmented, and in the process almost completely dehumanized, the role of people, it is not surprising that the reinstatement of 'people power' has sometimes been considered unimportant.

Another very important lesson learned from the introduction of computer integrated systems is that the companies that have used them most successfully have been those that were most successful in the pre-automation era. Their earlier success was in large part achieved by a high level of plant utilization. Training, motivation, organization and leadership of the complete workforce, at all levels, had led to a high utilization of plant investment. Their senior managements had recognized that investment in technology could only produce the desired results if the companies' employees and managements made it work. They never lost sight of the great importance of the human factor. For them it was more than a polite acknowledgement in a company annual report. Such companies were well prepared, when the time came, to introduce a new integrated technology, which was much less dependent quantitatively on human beings, but in qualitative terms much more so.

## A Pre-computer Revolution

Some firms have been lucky enough not to possess the considerable financial resources needed to plunge immediately into the new era of CIM. Before they could do so they were forced to reorganize their traditional ways of working, moving from the old linear workflow layout to gang operation of manufacturing cells. Necessity was the mother of innovation. Only by making such a fundamental change could the necessary strength be gained that was needed to enable them to move into the computer integrated age. Root and branch surgery was required that called for great courage from their managers. Perhaps the most traumatic effect was the collapsing of the multi-layered management hierarchy structures – quite often as many as five out of seven or eight layers were eliminated. At the factory floor level workers suffered a major cultural revolution as they were regrouped into interacting, cooperating teams and made responsible for their own productive output. It was a kind of rebirth in working life, and could only have taken place after extended periods of careful retraining in skills and personal preparation. Working again as part of a gang, employees unleashed a new creativity. Responsible people act responsibly when given responsibility. They act irresponsibly when they are denied the dignity of responsibility.

The results shocked many cynical managers as they realized just how much human talent, energy, commitment and ingenuity had been wasted under the old regime. For them faith in human nature was regained. It was not only the improved financial strength of such firms that enabled them to qualify for entry into CIM: the remaking of their workforces and managements was also a necessary precondition.

## Investing in People

Despite the increasingly capital-intensive nature of most businesses and the decrease in the labour element (particularly direct labour) we have still not broken the habit of seeing productivity in terms of output per worker. It is as though we were still operating in the age of hand tools and quill pens when there was no other form of productivity. One consequence of that unbroken habit is an investment imbalance. On the one hand investment has to be made in property, plant and working capital by the company; but it appears that no investment by the company is required in the other vital factor of production, the labour asset – despite the fact that the effective utilization of the material and financial assets of the company are entirely dependent on the labour element.

That odd asymmetry is understandable in the context of the deskilled worker system of Taylorism, in which tasks were so simple that an intelligent operator was unfit for the job. With the new approach to the organization of work the neglect of investment in the human factor of production is totally unacceptable from the points of view of both the individual and the company. Within the family of advanced industrial nations training investment is at its lowest in Britain. In the USA and Japan expenditure per unit of turnover is about six times greater, and currently runs at about 3 per cent. Other western European countries are not far behind. In the future, these higher levels of expenditure are more likely to increase than fall, despite the smaller numbers of employees involved per unit of turnover. They will certainly be a very significant proportion of the total annual financial investment, and should be seen as a part of capital investment rather than as an unrelated training cost.

## Training from the Top

New technology has very important implications for management training and formation. I learned one expensive lesson when, for a period, I was responsible for technical training courses for marketing staff – that its effectiveness was directly related to the level of understanding of the courses possessed by the trainees' managers. A great deal of money can be wasted in training front-line personnel if their managers do not know how to make best use of the knowledge, skills and experience gained on such courses. Training, like so much else, needs to begin at the top and, in a changing world, has become a continuing process. Even the most senior are not exempt.

The collapsing of hierarchical pyramids and the elimination of much of middle management open up a considerable communications gap between senior management and operating levels. This must be bridged. In the multi-levelled systems, the steps of understanding and knowledge were comparatively small and communication was consequently easy. In the absence of intermediate steps the problems of communication are more difficult. They require careful study and well-prepared methods, if transmission in both directions is to be clear and effective. It is a significant feature of the new situation that communication from lower to higher levels is at least as important as its counterpart. There is no longer any escape from total involvement and participation at all levels. Under the old regime senior managers were not only responsible for what work had to be done; they were also responsible for indicating *how* it must be done. Their messages were passed 'down the line' with detailed interpretation at each level. Increasingly senior managers are able to concentrate much more on the *what* than the *how*; methods are now largely the province of those people responsible at the 'action end'.

This does not mean that senior managers do not need a thorough grasp of the detailed workings of the business. On the contrary, they will need it more than ever before if there is to be effective communication with operators. In the past the existence of layers of experienced and knowledgeable intermediate managers allowed seniors with little real understanding of the detail of the business to get away with it. That will no longer be possible as the new technology replaces the intermediaries and senior staff have to communicate directly with operatives. The old notion that a successful senior executive in one business could manage any other business with equal success will no longer have any credibility in the age of post-Taylorism. It has only been the existence of competent intermediaries that has given the idea any credibility in the past.

From my personal experience I believe that, in Britain particularly, those senior managers who have not risen through the ranks from an operating level will need to take particular care to understand the culture of the shop floor, if communication is to be effective. On various occasions when employee relations problems have arisen I have been struck by the almost total lack of understanding, on the part of some senior managers, of the employee representatives' point of view. Much of the discussion in such circumstances is at cross purposes. That a culture gap exists in Britain, much more significant than any I have experienced in other European countries, was forcibly brought home to me when I visited two very similar plants, one in England, the other a French company of which I had recently become Chairman and Chief Executive. The purpose of my visits was to meet as many of the employees as possible. In the English plant I was met mostly by surly indifference; in France the work-force welcomed me with a champagne party! Overseas, we are beginning to realize the need to learn our foreign clients' languages, and to understand their different cultures. But here in the UK, while we may use the same words, our unfortunate culture gap so often gives them different meanings so that we convey different signals with them: it all depends on which part of the culture is ours.

## Creative Managers Needed

A feature of the development of businesses since World War II has been the increasing prominence of accountants in senior management positions. This was an understandable trend as a money-centred vision and set of values became dominant. If a business was perceived as a machine into which money was fed so that more emerged at the other end, it was not unreasonable that the machine should be managed by a money expert. The adding of money value will be no less a condition of company survival and fitness in the age of new technology. However, it is becoming clearer that in order to be successful with the application of information and other micro-electronic systems, senior managements must become more the conductors of orchestras, engaging in people-centred activity, than mere operators of money-making machines.

If accountants are to continue to play a leadership role it is unlikely to be mainly because of their knowledge of finance – just as few people would aspire to be successful symphony orchestra conductors because of their knowledge of acoustic physics. Accountants will, like all others, have to become fully acquainted with all the instruments and players in their orchestras if the melodies they conduct are to be harmonious.

## Arranging Things Differently

Having touched on some of the important consequences, for managers, of a shallow hierarchical pyramid structure brought about by the new technology, and the responsible and humanly enriching role of the resurrected gang system for people at the action end of business, we will now consider some of the other beneficial ways of reorganizing working life. There are two very important, albeit at present marginal, trends that are beginning to occur, which, within a few years, could lead to a revolution in the way that business affairs are conducted. These are the dispersal of operations and sub-contracting.

During my twenty-eight years of employment in Shell companies the world-wide business enjoyed an eightfold increase in activity. When I joined in 1946 the total number employed in the big oil operations and small, new chemicals business was well over 200,000 in about 100 countries. When I retired in 1974 employment had decreased to about 150,000, even though the chemicals business had grown to a considerable size, natural gas had become big business in some regions, a metals business had recently been acquired and a start was being made on an international coal operation. Despite the great increase in manpower productivity, frequent comparisons with other oil companies showed that their output per employee was lower, both on a company basis and on a location or plant basis. Invariably this discrepancy was almost entirely caused by the fact that we tended to do a great many more things 'in house' than some of our competitors. Although the Henry Ford idea of a self-contained, totally integrated plant idea started in the USA, it appeared that it had more influence on us than it had on American oil companies. There is nothing new about the sub-contracting of ancillary activities; indeed successful businesses like Marks & Spencer and Amstrad are examples of how even basic production can very effectively be sub-contracted by major, mature companies provided the necessary arrangements are made for *control* of those activities to remain with the companies. What *is* comparatively new is the geographical dispersal of some of the internal office activities that modern, rapid-communication, information systems make possible.

## Dispersed Office Work

Just as the experiment in work gangs at Volvo is often quoted as the prototype for this now fairly widespread method of organization for work on the factory shop floor, so the experiment at Xerox is seen as one of the pioneering moves in the development of 'dispersed offices'.

In 1982, as part of a fundamental examination of their organization in the light of new information and computer technologies, a decision was taken to set up an experimental group of office staff, including several senior people, as independent consultants with contractual arrangements which made the Rank Xerox Company a major client for a period of several years, with an open option for renewal thereafter.

The consultants' offices were equipped with terminal machines that were compatible with the Company's central communication and information network. It was possible to offer the consultants fees well above salary levels, and more than sufficient to cover the consultants' modest overheads. Thus the arrangement was financially attractive to the individuals so dispersed; but there were other attractions – the freedom of running their own small business, freedom from commuting daily and the ability to share more in the lives of their families. It was equally attractive to the Rank Xerox Company, which made substantial savings in the provision of office space and direct support services. In many such large companies located in major commercial centres, the total cost of employing someone is more than double the average salary paid.

Inevitably there are prices to be paid by both the company and the consultant. For the consultant these are associated with the loss of close relationships of a day-to-day kind that are, for many people, sources of great personal interest and satisfaction in working life. However, this loneliness factor can now, in many parts of the UK, be compensated for if the consultant works in one of the many low-rental, licensed, multi-occupation office blocks that are to be found in the new small business parks. The main loss for the company's management is the individual's comparative unavailability. But this is a small price to pay compared with the release from onerous obligations as an employer.

In the past it was not only in the Civil Service that the importance of a managerial position was measured by the number of subordinates employed. In the years to come it may well be that a manager will be more favourably judged if the number of company employees under his or her direct control is small. I recall the sense of shock when, as a division manager, I was asked to submit a proposal in which I was to increase my responsibilities substantially with a 50 per cent reduction of my directly employed staff. Three years later with the change completed, and even more responsibility than originally envisaged, I found it a considerable relief to be working with a smaller team, and with fewer non-essential distractions. There was no loss of effectiveness that I or any of my senior colleagues could detect.

I had acquired a taste for acting imaginatively, and presented a good case for further improvement and cost reduction. This involved the relocation of my whole Division to the country, away from the central offices, in order to be nearer to the main R&D laboratory people with whom we were close working partners. I now had a new superior who was, unfortunately, not as adventurous as his predecessor. Had he agreed to my proposal we might have been one of the pioneers of office dispersal.

## Sub-contracting

There remain the remnants of an old idea that if an activity is to be properly controlled it is necessary to employ all those engaged in it. Happily there is now so much experience that demonstrates its falsity that it is rapidly disappearing. Where it still continues to be recognized it is usually associated with an anachronistic management style of 'master and servant'. Although that style can still function in some very small organizations where the senior manager can be involved in every detail of the operation, there are few, if any, medium-size or large firms in which it can produce good results; and there are many situations in which even the smallest company is well advised seriously to consider sub-contracting quite important aspects of the business.

People counselling individuals who are planning new manufacturing ventures, often find that it is desirable to sub-contract, from the start, the actual production of the goods. Not only does this have an important advantage in substantially limiting the initial risk investment (which incidentally eases the nervousness of banks who are asked to provide loan capital); it also allows the entrepreneur to concentrate on developing a business rather than remain preoccupied with the time-consuming detail of manufacture. Many of the people setting up manufacturing businesses have a production background and little or no experience in marketing and general business affairs. In those circumstances sub-contracting the work you know best is a very great help in building up vital business experience.

There is a danger for managements of organizations, of any size, that contemplate sub-contracting. It can be a bad mistake to think that if it is sub-contracted there is no need to be as knowledgeable about the activity, nor as concerned with it, as would be the case if it were done 'in house'. For example, inadequate monitoring and control of sub-contracted manufacture in the automotive industry has had a very damaging effect on more than one company's reputation. Sub-contracting does not basically change management's responsibility for the activity. Detailed plans still have to be approved with the sub-contractor; a system of regular information, monitoring and control still has to be agreed and followed with such intervention as may from time to time be required. Means must also be provided for timely evaluation of the whole sub-contracted operation. Circumstances change with increasing speed. Within a comparatively short time it may be necessary to have a complete re-evaluation, particularly if the sub-contractor is unable to be as responsive to change as is required. The initial choice of a sub-contractor who will become a harmonious partner can be a difficult and time-consuming task. Although the best partnerships are frequently very intimate – the relationship between a firm like Marks & Spencer and one of its suppliers is no less intimate than one in an internal operation – they are not unchanging and they do not last for ever. Proper provision needs to be made to cope with unforeseeable changes and to allow for a mutually agreeable divorce.

## Negotiating a Sub-contract

The process of negotiating a good sub-contracting deal requires as much sensitivity as a major sale negotiation. I recall an occasion when a manufacturing manager returned from a meeting with a potential sub-contractor who had been very carefully selected. His mood was triumphant. He really felt that he had obtained every possible advantage from the agreement. When I asked whether he was satisfied that there was also advantage in it for our potential partner he looked rather nonplussed. His attempts to deal with the question convinced me that he had entered the negotiation in a belligerent way, determined to present me with a total victory. It may be that his mood was caused by his regret at losing direct 'in-house' control. I tried not to deflate him in his hour of triumph, but gradually brought him round to agree that it would be to our advantage, as well as to our partners', if he were to go back and suggest some worthwhile concessions.

I believe that far too little attention is paid in the business world to the importance of mutuality in relationships of all kinds. Too often there is a win–lose atmosphere that may sour a partnership; an imagined win can then turn out to be a loss. The best negotiations are the ones that produce a well-balanced set of benefits and sacrifices for both or all parties. As competition becomes keener we need to remind ourselves and colleagues that management is not a gladiatorial contest; it is, rather, a process which tries to ensure that all involved – customers, suppliers, sub-contractors, agents, employees, shareholders – are satisfied.

### Many Different Forms of Sub-contract

There are many different forms of sub-contracting. Each has advantages and disadvantages for a particular set of circumstances. There are licences to produce, licences to sell and licences to produce *and* sell, all with various terms and conditions. There is a wide range of agency arrangements and distributorships. Transport and warehousing can often be usefully and profitably contracted out. Many manufacturing firms purchase finished components made to a design that suits their requirements; others sub-contract the production of parts that they have designed. These options are available to companies of all sizes. In major oil company operations a wide range of sub-contracting methods are adopted in all the main functions of exploration and production: pipeline, rail, road and marine transportation, refining and marketing. A fascinating part of the management of marketing development in the international oil business was the variation, according to changes in market competition, of the mixture of the several sub-contracting schemes in each of the different market segments – agriculture, domestic, marine, aviation, automotive, industry and construction. For a company to have attempted to do all this itself would have been so rigid as to be disastrous. Sub-contracting provided amazing flexibility in the management of change.

A key to success in the management of a business living through a period of change is to remain as flexible as possible. That means making the best possible use of sub-contracting opportunities, while retaining full control of all those functions and decisions that a customer-orientated business is responsible for. With distractions minimized, it becomes possible with a small core group of very experienced and competent people to achieve a high level of business performance no matter how difficult the conditions.

### Influencing Sub-contractors

A large company is in a strong position to lay down conditions with sub-contractors that can ensure that high standards are maintained by them. This not only applies to the quality of the work and the level of service that must be provided; it can also apply to many aspects of a sub-contractor's operation, including the conditions of work and employment of its employees. As the role of major employing companies declines, the return of exploitation of employees by smaller companies is a serious worry. It is not in the interests of the general population, or of big companies or, of course, of the victims of exploitation that such conditions should be tolerated.

The influence that valued large companies can exert on small and medium-sized sub-contracting firms is probably the best influence that exists against exploitation. It should not be construed as bullying: if such influence is exercised it needs to be accompanied by high standards of treatment for the sub-contracting firm – including prompt payment of bills. What is sauce for the goose is sauce for the gander.

## Expectations and Attitudes

So far in this chapter we have considered some of the ways that the technological imperatives are likely, increasingly, to affect the structural arrangements for the conduct of work, and their important implications for managers. Next we must see in what ways these technologically driven rearrangements correspond with, or diverge from, the expectations and attitudes of most working people. The changes through which we are living are essentially taking place at a time when jobs have to be made to fit people rather than vice versa. Unless there is a very substantial measure of correspondence between new arrangements and the needs of working people the benefits of the new technologies will not be realized. We now return to the overriding importance of the human-machine interface.

The best-known model of a hierarchy of human needs (see figure 5.1) was described by Abraham Maslow.[1] He presents needs diagrammatically as layers within a pyramid standing on a broad base;

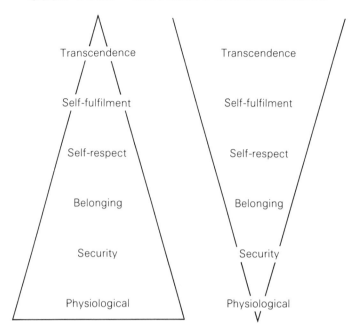

**Figure 5.1** Hierarchies of human needs: Abraham Maslow's diagram (left) and Kenneth Adams's version.

physiological needs are at the bottom and our need for transcendence and self-fulfilment at the top. It suggests that as we grow, progressively satisfying our needs in the order shown – physiological, security, belonging, self-respect, self-fulfilment, transcendence – our most basic needs are greater than the higher ones. For example, it suggests that our need for food and shelter is greater than our need for self-respect or self-fulfilment. Yet it is a matter of fact that our need for air, food, water and warmth is physically limited and our belonging needs and our security needs are fairly easily satisfied; but our higher needs – self-respect, self-fulfilment and transcendence – are limitless. I am very grateful to Kenneth Adams for an important insight concerning this pictorial representation. He suggests that an inverted pyramid would be a truer picture of reality.[2]

It is paradoxical that our understanding of the contribution made by employment to the satisfaction of human needs has been sharpened by the high levels of long-term unemployment in the 1980s. During the post-war years of full employment most people in Europe enjoyed marked improvements in their living conditions. As material prosperity grew so did general life expectations. At the same time as the lower needs became largely satisfied, so the unlimited non-material needs increased in importance.

## Job Satisfaction and Dissatisfaction

Widespread research amongst unemployed people in the mid 1980s certainly showed that there was a strong sense of money deprivation as a consequence of being without a job. But it was a special kind of money, earned money, that was missed, and no improvement in dole could replace it. The difference is that earned money is a reward for effort and also, in one way or another, is negotiated, whereas dole is felt to be a gratuity determined completely by the authority that provides it. However, other deprivations were even more strongly felt with the passage of time. A personal sense of identity, purpose and status are for most people, for better or worse, linked with their jobs. This is not, as is sometimes suggested, a comparatively recent phenomenon, associated with the Protestant work ethic. It clearly existed long before the Reformation as is evidenced by the use of employment throughout the ages to provide names – Smith, Baker, Miller, Carpenter and even Thatcher! The loss through unemployment of the very deep human needs of the senses of belonging, self-respect and self-fulfilment is probably the greatest loss of all; conversely it is employment that can provide those things for most people. Sadly, it also became clear from the experiences of a wide range of people that many of the jobs that people had occupied only provided a sense of belonging, with very little self-respect or self-fulfilment. Work had been fragmented into jobs that called for no real human contribution; they merely required unending, repetitive, simple tasks with little or no associated skill. Work failed to meet these most important human needs. Having lost such jobs, the dissatisfaction that people felt whilst they were still employed was greatly increased, so much so that some people vowed never to return to such dehumanizing work.

Although such jobs were by no means all in large, centralized companies, the experience of people who had jobs in small firms had been in many instances more satisfying and purposeful. Partly they could see more clearly the usefulness of their work; often it would be more varied in smaller firms, and there were opportunities to participate informally because of the much smaller division between the shop floor and senior management.

Undoubtedly the new technologies can, if properly used, make a very large impact, in firms of all sizes, in reducing jobs that provide little self-respect or self-fulfilment. Furthermore, by the changes in the way that the work of a company can be re-arranged through the various means of dispersion and sub-contracting discussed earlier, a great many more jobs could be in more satisfying, smaller organizations and far fewer correspondingly in big hierarchical institutions.

## The Loneliness of the Self-employed

Although in general there is a strong correspondence between people's present expectations, needs and attitudes, and a likelihood that such correspondence will continue in the coming decades, there are some aspects that will need to be carefully watched and arrangements made to address any adverse effects. Self-employment increased rapidly during the period of highest unemployment, with many of those choosing it coming from the ranks of the redundant. As unemployment began to decrease the proportion opting for self-employment has been maintained, with increasing numbers coming from people who already have jobs. Often the loss of social relationships enjoyed by those with jobs is keenly felt when the self-employment option is taken. I experienced this markedly when I retired from Shell in 1974 to work independently, promoting the adoption of 'appropriate technologies' and local enterprise trusts. Even though these two tasks put me in touch with fascinating people in the UK and abroad, there was initially nobody working with me with whom I could talk on a day-to-day basis, nobody with whom to share problems and ideas. Things improved markedly when I began to work with a colleague, even though we each worked from our separate homes forty miles apart. I believe that companies that engage the services of self-employed people will themselves benefit if some arrangement can be made for them to have easy contact with people in the office or factory; and some involvement is desirable in company meetings and events that would normally be attended if the self-employed person were an employee of the company.

## Managing Professionals

An organization restricted to a small number of professionals faces problems if it deals with a sub-contracted operational activity without the oversight of a core employee who has sufficient competence in the work sub-contracted. I recall a case in which a small, subsidiary, road maintenance contracting company had engaged a company of consulting engineers to create a new machine design for their own exclusive use. The contract had been in existence for almost a year, with inadequate contact between the company and the consultants. When I called for a progress report it was clear to me that the contract had to be cancelled immediately. The cause of the problem was that the company did not have on its staff an engineer with the necessary competence to initiate, monitor and control a machine design contract. It is important to understand that just because specialist consulting or other sub-contractors exist it is not necessarily appropriate to engage their services. There has to be within the organization at least one person with the necessary professional experience and ability to be effectively responsible. If such a person is not on the permanent payroll the need can sometimes be met through the engagement of a professional on a short-term contract.

At a time of great uncertainty and change the new age of innovative management is inevitably going to require a quantum leap in the management of professionals. It will call for qualities of leadership different from those that have been most common throughout the first Industrial Age. Before coming to an examination of reformed business leadership it is useful to note some problems that exist in running organizations made up of various professionals. Charles Handy mentions several.[3] Professionals in a group demand a great deal of autonomy, both in what they do and how they do it. They are as much and sometimes more concerned with advancement in their profession as they are in company status. They do not easily communicate with other types of professional. This places a considerable burden on anyone managing a mixed discipline group, and calls for exceptional tact and patience. It can be very difficult to stop professionals doing what they are doing, particularly if they have been doing it for a long time. They tend to avoid risk, and will often go to considerable lengths to avoid committing themselves to firm expressions of opinion.

Most professions have a body of knowledge which changes rapidly.

A professional can only remain effective if sufficient time and resources are provided that enable a high level of competence to be maintained. As professionalism increases investment of both time and money will have to increase for continuing education and retraining. This will inevitably build up pressures for democracy and involvement in policy-making. When management has to be by consent, how can management retain the exclusive right to manage? This trend towards an extended employment of professionals is already well under way. Until fairly recently, in my own profession, only graduate chartered engineers had a fully professional institution; now the technician grades are similarly organized.

In considering the correspondence between the likely, future rearrangement of work and the needs, expectations and attitudes of people, it is important not to lose sight of the necessity to compete with companies that put money first. I quote what is succinctly expressed in *The One Minute Manager* – 'How on earth can I get results if it's not through people . . . They go hand in hand . . . *people who feel good about themselves produce good results*'.[4] Happily, effective application of the new technologies and the different arrangements that will increasingly be required demands that business must and can be 'people orientated' – towards customers, employees, suppliers, sub-contractors and shareholders in the private sector, towards clients, suppliers and sub-contractors in the public sector. With technology and people well matched and working together harmoniously in a dispersed and flexible organization, innovative response to a rapidly changing environment should be swift and sure, but managements must always be concerned about their markets and look far enough ahead to see what is coming. Companies fail when there is a mismatch between their operations and the requirements of their customers. In the long run, no amount of juggling with figures will compensate for such a disharmony.

## Summary

As the age of the giant, entirely self-sufficient and excessively bureaucratic enterprise passes into history, a new world of work is being born. It is coming at a time when semi-skilled and unskilled jobs in most industries have disappeared. And it is also coming at a time when new Information Technology has opened up many exciting possibilities that satisfy two important desires. First, many skilled people wish to be more self-determining than they can be as full-time employees. Secondly managers need to be able to concentrate on the essentials of fast-changing, innovative business, and to be free from the distractions of supervising a wide range of essential but peripheral services.

The freedom created for managers provides the space for them to tackle the demands of a new 'people led' approach to the adoption of computer integrated business systems, and to handle the training and retraining of all grades of management and staff. However, the newly found freedom has to be matched by the development of different skills in the appointment, monitoring and control of the sub-contracting organizations that are replacing in-house service departments.

Even though the arrangement of work is undergoing radical change, the success of an enterprise will depend on the satisfaction of the increasing expectations and changed attitudes of all who are engaged in it. Although business is now great deal more technological the human contribution is also greater, not less, and leadership of people is the key requirement.

## Notes

* E. F. Schumacher, *Small is Beautiful*.
1  A. Maslow, *Motivation and Personality* and later in *Toward a Psychology of Being*.
2  K. Adams, Our Work and Our Faith. Tenth ICF Annual Lecture, Industrial Christian Fellowship, London, 1986.
3  C. Handy, *The Future of Work*. Basil Blackwell, Oxford, 1984.
4  K. Blanchard and S. Johnson, *The One Minute Manager*. Fontana, 1983.

# 6

# Conducting the Orchestra

Freedom and Order – this is the main organisational dilemma . . .
the funny thing is that when you lose one you lose both.

E. F. Schumacher*

With a corporate vision and set of agreed common values that is well thought out, with a clear idea of optimum size and appropriate work organisation, with a set of measuring instruments for planning, monitoring and controlling the operation, the successful management of innovative, sustainable development requires one more ingredient – an appropriate management style.

The main thrust of this chapter is to suggest that, in this emerging New Age of intense innovation management of business functions, at all levels, is going to be much more like the management of an R&D operation, or conducting an orchestra, than the 'machine model' management that has persisted throughout the twentieth century.

The 'machine model' perceived business as an essentially static operation, into which resources of people, money and machines had to be so introduced and controlled as to produce a higher value of output than input. It is of course a perfectly valid model in any age, and the orderliness and organizational disciplines that it requires are essential ingredients of any successful business. However, in an era of constant change the main emphasis in management was concerned with the administrative mechanics used to sustain and improve the smooth running of the business machine. It is perhaps no surprise that the most prestigious business educational qualification has been the MBA degree – master in business administration rather than management. It was also through that emphasis that accountancy and financial skills were given the highest rating, and the human aspects of motivation and creativity diminished in value.

Enough has been said in earlier chapters about the critical importance of the human factor in circumstances of discontinuous change. Although there can be no loss of orderliness and discipline, the operations of a company require a very different management attitude and approach if all available talents and energies are to be fully used. It is perhaps an unfair comment to say that managements have become, under the old 'machine model', more preoccupied with the score card – in business, with systems – than with the play and the players. Where the preoccupation has been excessive it has had a damaging effect on performance, as demoralizing gaps opened up between senior managers and other employees. With the need for greater flexibility and innovation, arising out of uncertainty and discontinuous change, the focus has to shift from the score card to the players and the play. This has always been the focus of attention in the management of R&D, and it is consequently the experience gained from that particular field of activity that can be of great value to all modern business managers. A wise manager with no experience of an R&D organization will be well advised to study books on the subject.

## Research and Development – What is the Difference?

In some ways it is unfortuante that research and development are intimately linked, thereby giving the impression that they are similar activities. In fact they are essentially quite different. Research aims at the acquisition of knowledge, and goes no further. Development aims at a particular concrete objective that is carefully defined – a product, a process or a system. The connecting link, of course, is that knowledge, which may in part be derived from research work, is a contributor to development. Some industrial or commercial development can take place without a supporting programme of research if the required information is already available. Some industrial or commercial research can take place entirely independently of a development project. However, it should not take place unless there is a recognizable potential connection with the strategy and policies of the business.

## Basic Research – Why Do It?

Research that is not in support of a particular development project is basic research. By no means all businesses engage in it; many believe that they cannot afford such a luxury. To perceive it as a luxury, in a period of unparalleled scientific and technological advance, is to misunderstand its nature and purpose. Even in companies that do take part in basic research, or that contribute to it in universities or independent research institutions, senior managements and their colleagues quite frequently have false expectations because they do not understand its real value to their companies. They falsely expect that the particular work into which they are putting money, time and effort should within a reasonable time lead to a major breakthrough that will, in turn, provide an opportunity for an important new business initiative. For example, a company sponsoring basic research in superconductivity phenomena may be hoping that the team they are backing will win the race for the discovery of the first commercially profitable superconductive materials. They may or may not be lucky. The trouble is that this is not the most important reason for sponsoring their team.

The main motive for companies to participate is that, by so doing, they gain access to the rapidly expanding field of open scientific and technological knowledge that is relevant to the future prosperity of their businesses. It is not an activity which has an identifiable return on investment; and it cannot be judged by concrete results achieved by some management deadline. Whether the money is well spent depends first on the quality of the leader of the research team, then on the value ascribed by the scientific community in their sphere of activity to the publications they produce. It is a waste of money to employ second-rate research workers and to deny high quality scientists the best equipment to work with. Every encouragement has to be given to basic research workers to publish their work: there can be no confidentiality. It is also important for them to take part in

---

Commitment, not control, produces results. The best and the brightest will gravitate towards those corporations that foster personal growth.

*Colin Southgate, Managing Director, Thorn–EMI*[1]

international conferences and make visits to meet scientists in other laboratories. Such a free and undirected life-style may be somewhat incompatible with other parts of the company; but to try to restrict it will certainly destroy its real potential value.

## Linking Management with Basic Research

However, the research team has to be well briefed as to the existing and future business interests of the company, and required to be constantly alert to the possibility that some new observation or discovery, wherever made, may be relevant to company interests. In order to ensure that this business orientation is maintained it is important that meetings take place, from time to time, between senior management and research workers. Senior managers must keep research workers informed about long-term plans and the strategies of the business. The researchers must alert their colleagues, in all parts of the business, to the effects that advances in science and technology will have upon it.

Investment in basic research is the price that is paid to be part of the network of scientists working at the leading edge in fields of vital business concern. A deliberate decision to remain outside that network is to forgo any possibility of either attaining or retaining a leading position. I can well recall losing the argument to become involved in fuel cell research in the early 1950s. Fortunately the decision was reversed two or three years later, and a very significant contribution was made by our team. A remark made by Lester C. Thurow, Dean of MIT's Sloan School of Management is well worth repeating: 'Once you start retreating, you end up retreating into oblivion.' The leading American business schools now realize that the manage-by-numbers skills they traditionally taught have left many US industries with people in important positions who do not understand research or technological innovation. There is a need to ensure that this does not happen to the new generation of European managers. But what of the small and medium-sized company that cannot have its own team of basic research staff? Some medium-sized ones may be able to take part in cooperative programmes, but those that cannot should nevertheless endeavour to keep an eye on progress in relevant fields of science and technology. It can be done by identifying particular technical people and sending them to important meetings, conferences and open days at research laboratories. I remember one such open day visit that had very beneficial results years after I had stopped working in a laboratory. For some time I had failed to interest colleagues involved in bituminous research into roads in the possibility of developing anti-skid road surfaces. While visiting the British Road Research Laboratory on an open day I noticed some results of studies on the resistance to polishing of a wide range of mineral aggregates. One, calcined bauxite, was outstanding. This chance observation provided me with the key to gaining the interest of colleagues. Confirmatory research and development and application work were put in hand. The outcome was SHELLGRIP, which over the past twenty years has been outstandingly successful in preventing death and injury at many car-accident black spots. Sir Alastair Pilkington, then head of Pilkington Brothers in St Helens, made a similar chance observation when visiting the British Building Research Establishment. This concerned the interaction of different types of glass and cement. One particular type of glass-cement combination was free from interaction. As a result a new family of glass-fibre-reinforced cements appeared from development made by Pilkington Brothers Research Laboratory. These two examples happened in large companies. The end result could have been the same had the individuals concerned been employees of small or medium-sized firms.

The reader will already be aware that the management of basic research is different from any other business activity. Many years ago the Director of Research of Kodak in the US wisely remarked that 'the one thing that a Director of Research must not do is to attempt to direct research.' The remark was made in the context of basic research. Once a first-class scientist has been recruited and a project agreed that engages his or her total enthusiasm, the management must show continuing interest, accepting that the work may change direction from time to time as the exploration proceeds. But there should be no interference. It is highly improbable that anyone will know better than the project leader what best to do next; and nobody need fear that a good scientist will want to persist if a particular line of enquiry is unproductive. So encouragement and genuine interest in the work are needed, but not interference.

## Applied Research is Different

It is safe to say that in every industry or business basic research will amount to no more in terms of expenditure than 10 per cent of the total investment in R&D. Most research work is applied; it provides specific data required for the development and design of particular products or processes, the characteristics of which have initially been carefully specified. Because it is narrowly directed research does not mean that it requires scientists, technologists and engineers any less able than those engaged in basic research. Many academics who mistakenly believe it to be an inferior type of work have learnt that it is usually just as demanding and challenging, and equally creative if not more so. Although some people prefer the unrestrained character of basic research, many gain satisfaction from problem-solving and a conclusion that is useful.

The applied research worker is one member of a project development team – whether or not the team is formally set up or is a loose association of contributors. He or she will be a good team member if the necessary teamwork discipline is agreeable and if there is the opportunity to participate fully in team decisions. Sometimes the special scientist is not so treated, but is regarded wrongly as a tame provider of information to order. Such treatment sells the company very short. Research workers have much more to contribute.

## 'Programme Management' and 'Project Management'

Essentially there are two levels of development management. They can be conveniently described as 'programme management' and 'project management.' During the long period of steady and continuous change the allocation of R&D resources to different areas of product and process development did not vary much from year to year. In many businesses most of the work was carried out in-house. Consequently, since R&D is essentially a human skill activity, the matching of the available personal skills of R&D staff with the gradually changing needs and opportunities of development did not present a very serious management problem. In a period of uncertainty and rapid discontinuous change the problem of management programme planning is far less comfortable. No longer may it be assumed that the basic company strategy will necessarily remain largely unchanged from year to year. Major changes in the particular business environment can occur with very little warning. Some contemporary examples come to mind. Food processing companies, for instance, have found themselves suddenly faced with a public revolt against food additives, after decades in which additives were a principal and increasing feature of their technological development. The nuclear power industry, after about thirty years of unhindered development, has been thwarted as a result of public fears. Major developments, such as fast reactors, are now in abeyance, and industry laboratories are increasingly having to look to other fields of activity in order to occupy the skills of their workers. With present uncertainties, each R&D programme planning activity must be preceded by a detailed and thorough review of the company's short-, medium- and long-term strategy and plans, with areas of uncertainty clearly identified and evaluated.

## Board Presentation of a Balanced Programme

R&D programme planning can then proceed in the light of the business strategy and plans review. When completed it can, as a result, be presented to the board in a form which makes clear the relationship between the various project elements of the programme and the business needs and opportunities. It is also helpful to a board if some indication can be given of the degree of technical risk involved in the different elements of the programme. It need be no more than a categorization into high, medium and low risk. Broadly speaking the highest risks are in projects that are 'technically led', that hope to make a major, innovating breakthrough. They are usually also the most commercially risky. The least risky are generally concerned with the gradual development of well-established products and processes. It is understandably exciting to contemplate a major high-tech breakthrough, but there is some worry that in Europe there is too much pursuit of such technology. Jean-Jacques Duby, IBM's European Director of Science and Technology has said 'In modern industry there is no such thing as high-tech and low-tech. You need all-tech to be competitive.'

The Japanese have a view on the most rewarding approach to innovation. NEC Corporation's Senior Vice-president and Research Director believes that innovation is 'the result of tiny improvements in a thousand places'. I recall the answer of the chairman of a European TV company when I asked why the Japanese had swept the world TV market. He said he could give no other reason than their amazing and continuous attention to detail in product and process R&D. The Director of the National Institute of Science and Technology Policy in Tokyo emphasizes the point, saying 'Revolutionary breakthroughs belong to an older paradigm. Today's paradigm for innovation is the fusion of different technologies.' The old, technical discipline barriers have to go. European company boards will be wise to consider carefully the balance, in their R&D programmes, between the big breakthrough part and the unglamorous 'tiny improvements in a thousand places' part.

The balance between product and process innovation also needs to be watched carefully. In Europe we have tended to follow the US pattern. There, over a very long period, there was a single-minded concentration on the achievement of low unit costs in manufacturing processes through long production runs. Even minor product innovations could upset that aim, so few resources were allocated to product development. As a result US manufacturing became inflexible and was caught off balance when the Japanese began to bombard the American market with a stream of increasingly better products. As we strive in Europe to be cost competitive across the world, we need to take care to focus on product development and at the same time ensure that manufacturing process development is providing great flexibility.


## A Technical Resource Dilemma

In most industries companies' own R&D laboratories have been traditionally manned with a comparatively narrow range of scientific and technological disciplines. With the fusion of technologies, and the rapidly increasing range of available materials, it is becoming more and more expensive and difficult for even the largest companies to maintain an R&D activity which is completely in-house. The problem is compounded as the balance of the programme shifts towards product development and is 'market led'. This quickly takes companies deep into the unfamiliar territory of their customers. I recall having to face this problem when Shell decided to examine the possibility of using oil products to improve the quality of metallurgical coke. Within the company we had no skills or facilities to deal with coking processes and testing. Fortunately we were able to set up a collaborative project with an independent coking research laboratory.

Although it is most likely that companies will continue to retain their own substantial R&D capabilities in appropriate areas, it seems probable that the range of different instruments that will be needed in the R&D orchestra will increase through greater use of sub-contracted work and the licensing of technology produced by independent research, development and design organizations. As sub-contracted work becomes a much more significant part of a company's development programme, it is likely that its own operation will find itself having to compete with independent organizations, even in the core technologies of its business. I can vouch from personal experience that it can be a considerable shock for a company project development team to be told that the process or product of an independent research organization is being taken by the company in preference to its own.

This is one among several reasons why it is increasingly necessary to separate the responsibility for the management of in-house resources of R&D from the responsibility for decisions about product and process innovation. Those decisions are essentially commercial with an important technical content, and they should be taken by the people who are accountable for the results of commercial exploitation. In the early 1960s Shell introduced the notion of the so-called 'customer–contractor' relationship between the business functions of manufacturing and marketing (customers) and the research directorate (contractor).

With that arrangement the director of research was solely accountable for the basic research programme. Although there was no support required from the marketing or manufacturing organizations, for any part of it, there was considerable mutual interest and contact. Applied research and development projects had to be jointly planned and paid for by the customer functions. The more it becomes necessary to engage the services of independent research laboratories the more valuable is this clear separation of responsibilities. It is very important that a talented R&D laboratory team takes a long time and a lot of money to develop. It cannot easily or quickly be changed, and it must be given every opportunity to exercise its talents and enthusiasm. Consequently the person in charge must be as free to sell spare laboratory capacity to outsiders as is the person responsible for development decisions and exploitation to buy work or license technology from outside sources. That freedom for the laboratory director will be of increasing value as the company innovation programme becomes more dynamic and variable, and as laboratory equipment and facilities become more capital-intensive. Both the laboratory plant and the workers need to be kept fully employed.

## How much R&D is Needed?

A short and general answer to the question is 'better too much than too little'. There are no formulae to guide decision-making; and it varies a great deal from industry to industry. It is a matter for careful and well-informed judgement: it is difficult to settle on precisely the right amount. Too much is better than too little because of two important considerations. Unless the programme is extremely pedestrian, with very little risk, it is not possible to be certain about the chances of success. With luck, a higher than expected success rate may be achieved, the only disadvantage being a short-term, marginal reduction in company net profit. If, on the other hand, with a very tight programme, all does not go according to plan, the consequences for a company may be much more serious later on. In some circumstances they may be disastrous. It is better to risk a little short-term profit loss than to hazard a company's longer-term prospects.

There is a widespread fallacy that traditional, well-established products require little R&D. This is certainly not so now that the availability of new materials, new production and control equipment and systems, and new technologies is increasing at such a rate. 'Tiny improvements in a thousand places' applies as much to well-established products as it does to those that are comparatively new. Failure to recognize this fact largely accounts for the comparative lack of competitiveness in much US and European traditional industry. Even in the most advanced industrialized economies, more than two-thirds of average household expenditure goes to purchase traditional products. David Foster estimated that only about 2 per cent of innovation expenditure in Britain was devoted to the products that ordinary people buy, whereas over 70 per cent was spent on capital goods.[2] Does this not suggest that money was being spent at a high rate on advanced manufacturing technology that was used to make out-of-date products? While this was happening, British industry's share of the market in domestic consumer goods fell dramatically in the face of imports preferred by customers. The same phenomenon would appear to be at the root of the US balance of trade crisis. After nearly thirty years of personal involvement with traditional oil product development, I retired knowing that there would be no reduction in the need and the opportunities for potentially profitable R&D. Unfortunately there were people in the industry who did not share my optimism, believing that a plateau had been reached. After fifteen years those needs and opportunities are greater than I imagined they could be.

Another consideration that bears on the amount of R&D thought to be appropriate is the capacity of the company to handle a good piece of development successfully. In a large company this is not an easy judgement to make because there may be departments in many operating subsidiaries to be considered. Sometimes it only requires the inability of one department to produce a poor result for the whole company. At any one time there are usually more project proposals than can usefully be handled, and choices have to be made. Among the various factors to be considered, the capacity for successful exploitation is of prime importance.

## Providing a Development Programme Framework

Planning a development programme demands more than a list of possible projects options, even if a considerable amount of information has been produced in support of each of them, even if each has been underwritten by commercial, production and finance functions. There needs to be a framework that will enable choices to be made in relation to the strategic thinking of the board about the development of the whole business. When the pace of scientific and technological progress was somewhat more leisurely than it is today, a scientific and technological input may not always have been necessary for the evolution of such thinking. It would be a foolish board that forms business strategy, today or in the future, without such an input from the very best sources available. Such a technical contribution will have marked influence on some vital aspects of the board's strategic view by helping to answer the following questions:

1  What market sectors or niches should be the focuses for the development of the business?
2  What technologies are available, or are becoming available, that are

likely to make significant contributions to the development of the business in selected markets?
3 What scientific discoveries have been made that could either become a threat to some important aspect of the business, or could provide a basis for a new business opportunity?
4 What parts of the existing product range, what particular products or services, have a questionable future that may suggest their possible withdrawal?
5 What mergers or acquisitions may be needed to reinforce the technical capability of the business?
6 What disinvestments may significantly reduce the company's technical capability if there is no replacement?

Answers to such questions, no matter how tentative and imprecise they may be, can provide a useful framework for the choice of project elements in programme planning.

## Keep Some Spare Capacity

The increasing capital intensity of manufacturing or production facilities and the acceleration in the pace of product and process change are two factors that make it necessary for R&D to give a high priority to plant flexibility and maintaining a high level of use.

There is more than one opinion about the desirability of manufacturing of marketing service work being undertaken by staff whose primary role is R&D. Some companies prefer to keep them organizationally apart. Where there is a steady and heavy load of fairly routine service work it is necessary and desirable to have dedicated laboratory facilities. However, senior management should understand that if the quality of work in such a laboratory is to be maintained at a high level, spare capacity is necessary to allow some research and development to take place. It may well be that as this type of service activity becomes increasingly automated staff will need to devote more time to non-service work.

The existence of special service laboratories should not, in my opinion, exclude all service work from R&D laboratories. My experience is that, as long as the amount did not exceed 10 per cent of the total research worker-hours there was no unwelcome interference with the progress of R&D projects. I am convinced that such work, can enhance the quality of laboratory R&D work provided it is carefully selected and allocated to the most appropriate individual worker. There are various ways laboratory workers may be given relevant personal contact and experience outside the laboratory. I believe that none is more beneficial than a fairly regular flow of service work that has arisen out of operational problems.

## Performing the Programme from the Rostrum

So far in this chapter we have only been concerned with the preparation of the programme for the R&D concert. Before going on to the performance of the works that have been selected, we should remember that, in comparison with business management in less uncertain times, much more time and attention is required in the planning of business development and R&D programmes. If effective and efficient performance is to be achieved there must be very thorough planning and preparation. The *performance* of the programme is certainly more fun, but it does not do to skimp the preparation. It is sometimes said that the industrial success of the Japanese owes much to the exceptional time, effort and detail they put into planning.

### Authoritarianism is Out

Management's understanding of the minute-by-minute conducting of the operation has changed considerably. In 1987, as Chairman of Food for Britain, Walter Goldsmith said 'Management is out of date now. We've had too much management and not enough leadership.'[3] Conducting the operation is essentially the leadership of a 'team-of-equals'. The quality of leadership depends fundamentally upon the existence of an intimate understanding and rapport between all members of the team. Until a team has achieved that it is no more than a group of individuals, all of whom may be excellent in themselves. One task of the leader is to select members of the team

Increasingly in the 1990s the investment is going to have to be in people.

*Bob Reid, Chairman and Chief Executive, Shell UK*

with care, remembering that some may be star individual performers but not good team players. This does not mean that all team members have to be of the same type: there needs to be plenty of variety. But they must be compatible. In less turbulent times there was plenty of opportunity for members to get to know each other. Now that the rate of change is greater there is often very little time available. Consequently, during the selection process extra attention must be paid to compatibility. The leader must know the members of his or her team personally, and be aware of their likes and dislikes, as well as their various qualities.

If the team is to perform as a team it will need a shared vision of the aims of the joint enterprise, and a sense of shared ownership in it. This is more than listening and talking. The process of sharing the vision is important in itself. It must be so arranged that there is a good chance that mutual respect develops between all members of the team including its leader. Naval training taught me that leadership is not given – it has to be earned. I was not surprised to read a remark by Sir John Harvey-Jones, an ex-Chairman of ICI and former submariner, that 'Leadership is a priceless gift that you earn from people who work with you; and you have continuously to earn that right.'[4] In this age of specialisms and complex interdisciplinary teams, authoritarianism has no place. The continuous earning of the right to lead is vital. The leader has to do more than get the project off to a good start. The conductor needs to be active on the rostrum until the last note, putting energy into the operation by encouraging and inspiring the players. I recall the late C. C. Pocock, when he was a Managing Director of Shell, saying that the most important characteristic of a manager is that he or she remains fully involved and committed to each task until it is fully completed. Once the concentration of the conductor lapses the music loses colour and becomes pedestrian. The same happens to any organization that lacks stimulation and encouragement from its leader.

## The Conductor Must Understand All the Instruments

There was a time when good managers could give detailed job instructions to each employee. That is clearly no longer possible in an organization that is increasingly made up of a variety of professional specialists. However, it is not possible to be an effective conductor of an orchestra unless one has an adequate knowledge of what each instrument can contribute and what its limitations are. In the same way, an effective business leader must have a sufficient grasp of the disciplines of specialist contributors to the business programme in order to ensure that they have an opportunity to make a good contribution. Early in my career as an associate director of research I became aware that some of the research engineers were not contributing as well as I believed they might. It was only when I realized that they did not adequately understand some of the chemistry that was involved in the project that I was able to intervene usefully. A short course for engineers in the relevant aspects of organic and physical chemistry had immediate benefits by allowing them to participate more fully with confidence. It has frequently happened in the past that project teams have not worked harmoniously together because their members did not sufficiently understand the specialist languages used by their colleagues. An important function of a manager leading a multi-disciplinary project is to be alert to such problems and to act as an interpreter and clarifier when those taking part do not understand the language being used.

> I think most of us are looking for a calling, not a job. Most of us, like the assembly line worker, have jobs that are too small for our spirit. Jobs are not big enough for people.
>
> *Nora Watson and Studs Terkel*

Worthwhile two-way communication is never an easy matter. It becomes very much more difficult when the participants are mixed, with widely differing interests and backgrounds. Few people are natural communicators, and sadly the education system has so far failed to develop this most fundamental human art. It has increasingly become a crucial skill for managers, and it is necessary that they make serious efforts to develop it. Michael Faraday achieved a reputation as an outstanding lecturer and communicator during his time at the Royal Institution in Albemarle Street, London. He was not only a self-taught scientist and craftsman, but also a self-trained communicator. As a young man he recognized that he was unskilled in both the spoken and the written word. He spent five years studying in order to make himself a master of the art before he began his famous lectures.

**Encouraging Openness**

One serious hindrance to effective communication in business is the reluctance to say something that may be considered wrong. Cards are kept unnecessarily close to the chest for fear of playing a wrong one: better to keep quiet than run the risk. When that fear is common it is because managers have failed to encourage a tolerant spirit of openness. You cannot have openness without tolerance. It does not matter how unpopular opinions may be; people must feel free to express themselves. As a manager it is not at all easy to welcome criticism from subordinates and colleagues. However, unless criticism without rancour is invited and encouraged free and open expression in general cannot be expected.

> Management style is fundamental. People who lead from the front are likely to get support. Those who send messages from the front office are likely to get raspberries.
>
> *Roy Grantham, General Secretary of APEX*[5]

When leading a multi-disciplinary group, if time is short and precious, it is tempting to save it by holding discussions exclusively in groups. The concept of 'walking the floor', which has been well promoted by British Industrial Society is a good one. When I worked as a manager in a laboratory most of my time was spent productively doing this. But when I left laboratory life to work in a large office environment I found it was much harder to find time to wander from office to office, and somehow it did not seem to be the best use of time. I wish now that I had relied less on meetings and conferences, and had spent more time just wandering around. All my experience makes me agree with Tom Peters's idea of MBWA – Managing By Wandering About. My observations tell me that the best business 'orchestra conductors' are the ones that manage in this way. It is more than simply walking the floor in the factory, shop or office, meeting working colleagues. The wandering needs to take place both inside and outside the company. There needs to be personal contact with customers, suppliers, sub-contractors and others not directly connected with the business. Without the stimulus of the outside world it is virtually impossible to remain an effective innovative manager. In discussing the activities of basic research workers I stressed the importance of the conferences that they attend all over the world, and the visits that they make to other scientists. It is just as important for managers, if they are to be as innovative as they need to be, to 'wander about' widely.

In this chapter I have drawn from my own experience and that of other managers of R&D, as well as from lessons learned as a marketing and general business manager and company chairman. Just as R&D depends entirely on the leader's harmonization of the efforts and talents of individual project team members, so in an innovative business that is inventing and developing its own future managers will need to follow much the same principles as successful R&D managers have done in the past.

## Summary

That finance is the only essential knowledge required by senior managers is a common myth; consequently someone who has been successful as a senior manager in one particular business is thought to be capable of being equally successful in any other. Another is that management must manage in the same way that a general commands an army. Both these myths are anathema in the New Age of managing for sustainable development. The 'orchestra conductor' model of management requires an intimate understanding of a particular piece of music (the essentials of a particular business), a knowledge of each instrument (specialist function), the confidence of players in the conductor and the ability of the conductor to communicate creatively with all the players (mutual respect between managers and staff).

Modern businesses are becoming more like orchestras than armies as they incorporate more specialized technologies. For many managers following the military model a change of management style is required. A personality transplant is not necessary; it is something that can be learned by observing those who have already had to change – for example managers of R&D – and by 'Managing By Wandering About' with a determination to learn from the experience.

## Notes

* G. Kirk, ed., *Schumacher on Energy*.
1 C. Southgate, quoted in Clutterbuck and Crainer, *The Decline and Rise of British Industry*. W. H. Allen/Mercury Books, 1987.

2 D. Foster, *Innovation and Employment*. Pergamon, 1980.
3 W. Goldsmith, quoted in Clutterbuck and Crainer, *The Decline and Rise of British Industry*.
4 J. Harvey-Jones, *Making it Happen*.
5 R. Grantham, quoted in Clutterbuck and Crainer, *The Decline and Rise of British Industry*.

# 7

# Pulling Together – Alternative Ownership

*The problem is to find some principle of justice upon which human association for the production of wealth can be founded.*

R. H. Tawney*

The relevance of corporate ownership and constitution to sustainable development is less immediately apparent than that of the topics of the other chapters. At the deepest level the choice to move in the direction of sustainable development is a moral one. Expressed most directly, it is the choice between 'eat, drink and be merry for tomorrow we die' and 'live responsibly so that others may live'. To quote Margaret Thatcher, a consequence of the choice is for 'growth which does not plunder the planet today and leave our children to deal with the consequences tomorrow'.[1] It is a commitment to principles of natural moral law – equity, mutuality and justice. For sustainable development to be successfully put into practice, businesses which are the agents of economic development should be based on the same natural moral principles.

For the past hundred years and more the debate about the ownership of the means of production, distribution and exchange has been about public versus private enterprise. It has been a very limited argument in which little space has been left for consideration of alternatives. As some of the unacceptable faces of both socialist and capitalist systems have become inescapable, dissatisfaction with both, as so far practised, has awakened a desire to explore alternatives. This is now a realistic exercise at both theoretical and experimental levels, because a role for the market is universally acceptable, even in many communist countries. No longer is our choice limited to central control through state ownership or free market with private ownership.

In the non-communist world fundamental questioning is rife. The traditional assumption that the joint-stock limited liability company is the most perfect form of wealth-creating enterprise is being debated. The longer we live with it the more unsatisfactory it seems to be. Fortunately there are sufficient variations on the theme and forms of constitution to make it possible and worth while to explore in this chapter alternative ways of acting corporately that can contribute to the more plural form of economic life emerging today.

## Absentee Landlord Owners Dehumanize

There is a fundamental concern about the effects on people of working in joint-stock companies. Another concern is that they enable shareholders to accumulate unlimited wealth without any participation in the wealth-creating activity, but with the power to buy or sell such companies like any other piece of property. First, because such a company is, according to law, a piece of property, it has owners who can dispose of their property as they please without consultation or approval by anyone. As property owners they are at liberty, if they wish, to destroy the property. Consequently those whose working lives are devoted to the well-being of the Company — employee directors, managers and the rest of the work-force — are legitimately bought and sold at the whim of owners and for their personal gain. In this sense they are in a position not very different from that of slaves who, until slavery was legally abolished, were bought and sold for profit, with no say in the transaction or its terms. The insignificance of such employees is confirmed by the facts that, unlike the machinery that they operate, no payment is made to them when they join a company and their essential value to the company is not recorded in the balance sheet assets. In this latter sense they do not exist. Only a mysterious asset called goodwill to some extent reflects their value. Little wonder that a central complaint of Marxists is that capitalism views people as equal in value to land. Whether that is better or worse than viewing them as factors of production I do not wish to debate here.

Most of the owners of companies are no longer individuals or families. They have largely become the property of financial institutions, some of which represent many thousands of anonymous individual investors. As others play games with 'junk-bonds' and other spurious speculation, the whole concept of company ownership has come into serious question.

## Ownership Obligations and Rights

Before the introduction of limited liability, incorporation was granted for public benefit rather than for the private gain of the owner. Thus the owner, who took the entire financial risk of the enterprise, was also accountable publicly. The rights of ownership were inextricably linked with obligations.

With the introduction of limited liability, not only was the owner personally freed of much of the risk, but also the link between rights and obligations was broken. Because of the imbalance caused by the removal of legal obligations and public accountability, there has inevitably been a gradual increase in legislation aimed at replacing individual conscience – in matters such as product liability, consumer protection, disclosure, the health and safety of employees and environmental protection. A great deal of financial legislation has also been necessary. Much of this legislation has been designed primarily with large companies in mind, because of the serious and widespread consequences of any possible irresponsibility on their part. Unfortunately, through its very specific nature and universal application, this mass of legislation can frequently be very damaging – and sometimes impossible to implement – for small firms.

## Ownership and Natural Justice

However, the growing amount of legislation and regulation has done nothing to change the fundamental, property-based relationship between employer and employee – including managers and executive directors. Those who argue against a fundamental change point to the remarkable results which the admittedly imperfect system is still producing. No doubt there were considerable benefits for some people in the operation of the slavery system, but the argument for abolition was a moral one. The argument for a reform of the present ownership system also has an important moral dimension. It bears on natural justice and the dignity of human beings; but its other amoral and practical dimensions could offer further improvements in the operation and performance of companies in the New Age that the traditional system of ownership is very unlikely to provide.

The old ownership system worked most effectively in a hierarchical, authoritarian society in which a large proportion of the workforce were ill-educated, unskilled or semi-skilled, compliant people. With the gradual winding down of hierarchical business organization, with the replacement of authoritarian direction and management by leaders of the 'orchestra conductor' type, and with the increase in highly-skilled, multidisciplinary, pluralistic work-forces and organizational systems that were described in earlier chapters, new forms of company constitution and legal form will be required.

They will be forms that eliminate the sub-human nature of employment in the existing ownership system, and that prevent the buying and selling of companies as pieces of property without the full participation of all employees in the transaction. They will be forms that view a company not primarily as a piece of property, but as a responsible community of equal stakeholders that is publicly accountable. A community is not owned by anyone – neither legally nor financially. On the contrary, its members belong to it and they owe their loyalty and allegiance to it and to each other.

As Schumacher so elegantly argued, 'no system . . . stands on its own feet: it is invariably built on a metaphysical foundation, that is to say, upon man's basic outlook on life, its meaning and its purpose.'[2] Our basic outlook on life – as shown by the various elements of the paradigm change discussed in this book – is changing in many important ways. It is reasonable, therefore, to expect that there should be fundamental changes in the way business is perceived, constituted and organized.

## State Capitalism – Demonstrably an Unsatisfactory Alternative

Before we consider specific alternative systems to private ownership, as it currently exists, we should consider public ownership in the form of state capitalism as it has been applied in Western European countries. If an exception is made of public utilities such as water and sewage disposal, there remains little (and a diminishing) enthusiasm across the main political spectrum for state ownership of large scale industrial enterprises. This is not because such enterprises are intrinsically inferior in their capacity to generate wealth efficiently – indeed there are numerous examples showing that they can be at least the equals of privately owned companies in the same businesses. However, state control, through ownership, has frequently prevented firms from achieving their real potential because they have become constrained by arbitrary, political interference. Boards are not free to raise money, invest and use their added-value surpluses in ways they think are most beneficial to the long-term future of their enterprises. The short-term horizons of politicians are often at variance with the long-term needs of a business.

## Reformed Private Ownership

R. H. Tawney made a very important point when he wrote 'For it is not private ownership, but private ownership divorced from work, which is corrupting to the principle of industry.' Companies whose owners are actively involved day by day in their management and operation are nearly always small-scale and based in a local community. Invariably the owners of such companies take the financial risk, and they share the employment risk with all the employees, with whom they have close working relationships. It is perfectly reasonable that such an individual should take whatever surplus or loss there may be after all claims on the profits including his personal salary, have been paid. I believe that it is very important to recognize the general fairness of this particular example of privately owned free enterprise, providing as it does a model for all sizes of company – small, medium and large.

Personal experience, through my involvement with local enterprise trusts and agencies, has confirmed my earlier belief that a distinction needs to be made between the legal status of established small firms and that of free-standing companies younger than five years old. There is an 'infant mortality factor' in the lives of free-standing new enterprises. The risk of failure is highest in the first two years, during which few firms reach a healthy profit level. The risk then decreases, and levels out after five years. The risk of failure is made unnecessarily high for both the owner and the employees if the new company is subjected to all of the demands placed on its mature relations. As, in the New Age, the role of the small business increases, colouring local communities with their diversity and innovative quality, it is more important than before that their creation and survival should not be obstructed. (There will be further discussion in chapter 9.)

## More Scope for Employee Buy-outs

There is something more to be said about mature yet growing small companies. In recent years much of their value has been lost as a result of take-overs by bigger concerns. In many instances, as with local bakeries, flour-mills and breweries, closure has rapidly followed transfer of ownership. In other cases they have become less effective as they have become submerged in their new parent companies and their bureaucracy. It is perfectly reasonable that the original owner should be free to part with his or her brain-child and obtain an acceptable financial reward in exchange. However, the business will have been built in collaboration with the employees. To be fair to them, particularly to those with considerable service, the employees should be given the right by law to match an offer made by a potential purchaser. It is encouraging that, in recent years, there has been a remarkable increase in buy-outs by managers and by employees. Many of these have been acquisitions of the subsidiaries of large companies, but some have been, as in the case of the National Freight Corporation, of the large company itself. Whenever a transfer of ownership is taking place in an owner-managed company, an option for employees to purchase it would do much to create a feeling of job ownership amongst many small, family firms.

In some of the larger family firms, employing about fifty people or more, it is not unusual for important members of staff to be appointed as executive directors alongside representatives of the family. I became an independent, non-executive director in one such firm, by invitation of the family, and felt that other executive directors who were not members of the family did not contribute as they could or should even though the board chairman made every effort to draw them out. I knew from informal conversations with them that some of their views were critical of the company. Unfortunately these views were not being expressed and debated by the board. I can only guess that, as old and loyal servants, they did not relish a conflict with the family, particularly as they had no substantial personal equity investment at risk.

Unless means can be found whereby such executive directors can be enabled to function effectively as board members, it is probably better that they should not be appointed. They can probably make a more useful contribution in their roles as departmental managers, making their views known freely to the managing director, without the inhibition that comes with board membership. I have for a long time taken the view that there is only one good reason for appointment to board membership. It is that the appointee has a special, useful contribution to make to critical decisions. Clearly a board is vulnerable if it has little executive experience. However, it is also of little value if executive members are, for whatever reason, inhibited. I believe that it is unwise for senior members of staff to be rewarded with board membership for long, loyal and distinguished service alone. Distinguished service as a manager is not necessarily a good qualification for board membership in companies of any size.

Although it seems probable that self-employment, as well as small firms of many different kinds, will increase in numbers and influence, large and medium-sized joint stock companies will continue to be a very important part of the European economy for a long time to come. It is in this type of company that problems occur arising from the separation of ownership and personal participation in the creation of wealth – so-called 'absentee landlord' problems.

## A New Philosophy of Ownership

I did not recognize the importance of the legal constitution of companies, or of written statements of purpose and codes of intended practice, until in the mid 1960s Shell UK set up an employee relations planning group. It was assisted by the Tavistock Institute of Human Relations, and its purpose was to improve relations, and thereby increase productivity. The diagnosis was the existence of deep distrust and suspicion between management and unions. The treatment, which proved to be remarkably successful, was no more complicated than a formulation of company principles and objectives that was reviewed, criticized, modified and finally agreed by the work-force, the unions and the management. With a close personal knowledge of my colleagues in Shell UK, not only was I full of admiration for their agreement to the statement, but I was also convinced that they would implement it. Without that commitment such a statement could prove a disaster.

Bearing in mind that UK company law assumes that equity shareholders, and they alone, have the privileged right to expect that their business will be run to maximize the return on their investment, it was remarkable to read the formulation of company objectives stating that the optimization of all the resources used in the business was the aim. No less remarkable was the reason given for that commitment, which said 'Shell does not regard itself as owning these resources, but as holding them in trust to make the best possible use of them on behalf of the community.' It seemed an extraordinary statement, certainly at the time. The company does not consider itself to enjoy absolute rights of ownership of the resources that it has paid for. Instead it sees itself as exercising the duties, rather than rights, of a trustee acting on behalf of the whole community. However, in acting as a trustee, it is bound to do the best it can for all the people involved in the business in a just and equitable way. It must also pay proper regard to community needs and its environment, whilst at the same time creating monetary wealth at a rate, that not only covers all these requirements, but produces surpluses that will make further development possible, both in the company and in society. I was elated by this corporate statement of purpose, which I saw as a marvellous, modern interpretation of what is meant by Christian stewardship. Assets of all kinds were not owned absolutely but conditionally. Economic efficiency in the business was not to serve the purpose of enriching one part of the community – equity shareholders who were absentee landlords – at the expense of the rest. It was for the well-being of all.

In the years that followed the enthusiastic acceptance of the commitment by all concerned, and only because it was believed and put into practice, human relations and productivity markedly improved. The story of this important event is told by Paul Hill,[3] who was a leading member of the planning group.

## A New Legal Framework

Because I was so impressed by what had happened in Shell UK, I paid no further attention to the question of ownership until I started to become acquainted with George Goyder's ideas.[4] Under the influence of his wise and scholarly treatment of the subject I gradually came to see that the benefits of Shell's new philosophy of management could not be fully realized as long as the unjust legal position of companies in the UK remained unchanged. I can do no better than to repeat here what to me are the main points in his argument.

To begin with, in a company – which is the focus of the work and service of the community – people must be able to enjoy freedom and dignity, and not merely an income, if democracy is to survive and flourish. Company law must provide the framework that provides a right to freedom and dignity as well as a fair reward. Only then will it command the support and enthusiasm of the whole society, because it will be seen to be a unifying and just arrangement that enables everyone to pull together for the common good. The UK Company Acts, from 1855, embraced a concept that put private gain on a pedestal: the law needs to take us beyond this and become one that broadly defines the social responsibility of companies.

## Legally Shareholders are not Part-owners

Before coming to a discussion of the basic principles on which such a law might be drafted, George Goyder draws attention to the fundamental and cardinal distinction between a company and its equity shareholders. Lord Justice Evershed said that 'shareholders are not in the eye of the law part-owners of the undertaking. The undertaking is something different from the totality of its shareholders.'[5] Thus it is wrong to think of a company as being owned by its shareholders: they are privileged creditors of the company with certain defined rights, including that of selling their interest in the company. In a strictly legal sense the common belief that I own, because of my equity shares in Shell, a small piece of that company is mistaken; but I am not mistaken about my rights and duties as a shareholder. Personal responsibility will always be at a discount in a large enterprise so long as it is seen as being under the control of agents of outside interests, whether those interests be those of private shareholders, financial institutions or government departments. Every employee seeks the 'ownership of the job', with the security that goes with it.

Having disposed of the myth of shareholder ownership, we are free to consider what principles should support a law defining the broad,

> The best people want a sense of ownership. Authoritarian management is being replaced by networking, requiring an approach of greater consensus and diplomacy.
>
> *Colin Southgate, Managing Director, Thorn-EMI*[6]

social responsibility of the company citizen. There seems to be no good reason for thinking that the principles applying to a company citizen need be different from those governing the relationship between individuals and their communities. These are the principles of natural law, based on equality, justice and trusteeship. Natural law, according to the moral philosopher and economist Adam Smith, has mutuality as its cardinal principle. Businesses need to conform to that law and be in harmony with that principle. The influence of the market can be trusted only when it is serving a moral agent. In Adam Smith's time the moral agent was the family. In the age of large national and multinational companies, they must also be moral agents, companies accountable to society and accountable for their trusteeship in the use of resources loaned to them by the commonwealth.

## A General Purpose Clause

The consequences of the fundamental change that is proposed in the legal form of a joint stock company become of even greater significance for the New Age that we are entering. Within these advanced technology industries the informal authority of knowledge and skill possessed by a widening range of specialists, who may be employees or contractors, has to be aligned with the formal authority of management decision if the company is to be effective and efficient. Under the existing legal form, the alignment of these two kinds of authority is entirely dependent upon the benevolence of managers, because the business is not seen as a community of equals playing a team game with a common purpose. Without a new legal form that brings together these two kinds of authority, informal and formal, divisions and strife will increase. A new company constitution will require that directors and managers have a legal duty to use authority, balancing the conflicting interests of the many stakeholders, including society and the environment: the interests of the shareholders will not be pre-eminent. A good manager currently strives to maintain that balance, but is hindered by existing UK company law. The requirement to maintain that balance provides the basis of a general purpose clause in a new legal foundation.

*Five Elements of a Draft General Purpose Clause, proposed by George Goyder*[7]

1 Survival and growth the primary objects.
2 Customer satisfaction a priority, through the excellence of product and services.
3 Provision of the best possible work environment for employees as equal members of the company.
4 Shareholder rights, duties and interests.
5 Responsible citizenship duties to government, local authorities, the environment etc.

The interpretation of the general purpose clause will need to be made by each individual board in consultation with the management and work-force. In some elements standards and codes of practice will have to be established by agreement, and performance will have to be monitored against them. The way added value is to be divided between stakeholders will usually be an issue to be considered. Charles Handy gives the interesting example of the Devon-based china and ball clay mining group Watts, Blake and Bearne.[8] Each year it says in advance how it intends to distribute added value, with a promise to give employees, say, 60 per cent if this turns out at the end of the year to be greater than the percentage they have received in their pay packets and salary cheques. In effect they publicly plan a distribution to employees of part of any residual surplus that may be produced.

## Corporate Citizenship

Citizenship duties will obviously present a considerable problem for most large companies. Vague expressions are inadequate but, because there are no limits, citizen duty is quite naturally feared by managers as a potentially serious distraction from the primary objects of survival and growth. However, choices have to be made.

In the US employees are widely encouraged to play an active part in their domestic communities. The general spirit and morale of a community in which a company has substantial operations is a matter of concern for its management. I came across this several times, in such companies as ICI, British Steel, Pilkington Brothers and Johnson & Johnson, when I was involved in the initial promotion and development of local enterprise trusts. Part of the motivation of several companies with which I worked, companies which made a commitment to participate in these partnerships between private and public sectors, was to improve the local morale and spirit.

Another motive was to show mutuality. It was well expressed in a speech by my late Shell colleague C. C. Pocock who said 'I believe that big companies should establish a positive policy which recognizes the value of small enterprises . . . and resolve to support this in action.' Shell has certainly lived up to that resolve. These examples are valuable because so often managements do not make a clear distinction between the things private individuals can do as expressions of citizenship and those that companies can do. If they do not, contributions may be made to all kinds of diverse (though worthy) causes which have no obvious relationship to the company's capacity or interests, but are rather the personal preferences of the directors. The choice of how a company may best express its corporate citizenship rests on what it has to offer to meet those needs that have a clear relationship to its interests.

Links with schools and colleges are an obvious example. Through my experience as an active member of the Chartered Engineers UNCLE project, in which I have enjoyed working with technology teachers in two Dorset schools, I have become convinced that there is a great deal to be gained by schools *and* companies – if firms encourage employees to give a little time – say an hour or so a week in term time – to visit schools and work alongside teachers, and if schools encourage teachers to spend time in companies.

## New Institutional Arrangements

The kind of fundamental constitutional change that has been described requires new institutional arrangements to channel power and ensure accountability. A very important relationship that must be revised is the one between companies and trade unions that have bargaining rights, staff associations, and works councils. There will be a need to consider the reconstruction of boards to provide a voice for interests that, under the existing regime, are excluded. It may also provide an opportunity to see whether there might be some benefit to be derived from a two-tier board system. Inevitably annual general meetings can never again be for shareholders only, and the broader span of a company's membership will call for a much more comprehensive and open report from its board than those which have traditionally focused on financial performance and prospects. The scope of independent auditing will need to be extended beyond finance. It will need to include the change of state of the human resources and the material, technological and scientific resources. Environmental performance and citizenship will also require an independent social assessment.

However, the exercise will not be complete as long as there remain rights that allow people, families, trusts and institutions to hold equity shares in perpetuity. Goyder writes 'It is iniquitous to give control over an organization dependent upon the daily cooperation of free men and women to absentee landlords from now until doomsday. We must chose between perpetual equity and freedom, for the two are in the long run incompatible'.[9] They are incompatible because they are contrary to natural law, the cardinal principle of which is mutuality. Until company law has been fundamentally changed to make equity shares in public companies subject to defined termination, the underlying discrepancy in purpose between employees' and shareholders' interests can be partially reduced by making employees voting members of a company and setting up a trust fund to hold shares on their behalf. Since 1982 British companies have been allowed to buy their own shares and some, along with some American companies, have taken this step. But the fundamental wrong will remain until a law is introduced that will ensure that equity shares are regularly redeemed on termination at their market value, so that a company may eventually become a self-controlling and self-disciplining economic and social organism, fulfilling the corporate purpose set out in its memorandum. In other words the large public joint stock company must be converted into a public trust, with directors who are charged with the responsibility of seeing that the terms of the trust are carried out to the best of their ability.

One of the growing weaknesses of the free enterprise system is the decline in sources of risk capital for new, free-standing ventures. If there is to be the amount of dynamic innovation that this paradigm change should produce, there is likely to be a growing need for such money, both for initial investment and for the early expansion of firms, which may be almost equally risky. Termination and redemption of mature equity shares, which generally no longer bear much risk, should free money for alternative investment. Some of it should find a home in new ventures where the risks and potential rewards are higher.

The giant corporations have so increased their power and influence in the past century that they have become rather like the barons of old − determining where we live, where and when and how we work, and for what objectives. There will, of course, be great resistance to radical change from vested interests. However many of these changes, are making the present legal position more and more untenable, and they will continue to do so. A charter for industrial and commercial democracy seems inevitable.

## Preventing the Problem in the First Place

The problem of the joint stock company does not arise, of course, if the original owner decides against conversion to a public company in the first place. Conversion into other forms of constitution goes back a long way. In 1896 Karl Abbe, the founder of the famous Zeiss optics company in Germany, gave the firm to its work-force through the formation of the Karl Zeiss Foundation of Jena. The articles of trust in its generous constitution have remained intact − even after East Germany became a communist state. For example, employees are encouraged with automatic leave of absence and full pay, to stand for election to official positions in the community. An early example in Britain was the formation in 1929 of the John Lewis partnership. This major, London-based retail store became entirely employee owned; since then it has grown into a flourishing nation-wide group. In 1982 the National Freight Corporation was acquired by its employees and has since flourished. However, its legal status did not prevent its new owners from selling their shares to outsiders, so it cannot be considered to be fundamentally different from any other joint stock company.

A recent and much more interesting example is Richard Baxendale & Sons Ltd. of Bamber Bridge, Preston, the producers of the Baxi range of heating appliances. The company was founded in 1866 by the great-grandfather of the present chairman, Philip Baxendale. Its success was based on the excellent Baxi patent coal fire, invented by Philip's father. Under the leadership of the present chairman, very rapid growth occurred between 1955 and 1983, largely owing to its success in capturing a 20 per cent share of the market in domestic, gas-fired heating appliances. By 1983 it was employing 900 people with a turnover of £37m. During that period of rapid growth Baxendale, closely supported by a colleague, Ian Smith, paid particular attention to the involvement and participation of employees, in order to retain the good relations and spirit of common endeavour that had existed when the firm was much smaller. Having achieved a high degree of participation, the family owners were loath either to sell their company to a willing buyer – who would probably have been a competitor – or to convert it to a public corporation. After a long and very detailed study of alternatives to these two conventional courses of action, the decision was taken to move from participation to partnership.

## A Partnership Company

I cannot do better than quote Baxendale's own words.[10]

I feel very strongly that I could not sell my share in Baxi to the highest bidder and not care what happened to the Company and the people in it. I also believe that the Company is not mine to sell, certainly not in the sense that I would sell a car or a house . . . we have now come up with a method which enables the Company to pay the shareholders a price they are prepared to accept and which the Company can afford to pay. The Company will then be owned by an Employee Trust. Ultimately it will be owned, the majority by the Trustees, and up to 49% by the Partners as individual employees.

In the well-established tradition of Baxi participation, details of how the partnership is to work is a matter for discussion between the partners and the trustees. The partners will own shares as individuals so that they will have a stake in the profits that are ploughed back. The shares will pay little, if any, dividend, but they will appreciate in value in line with that of the company. Employees will be able to cash them all in on retirement, and some may be able to cash some in while still in employment with the company. Thus the ownership is partly collective – the 51 per cent majority trust – and partly individual members of the work-force. The collective element ensures that the long-term interests of the partnership as a whole are taken fully into account. Furthermore, none of the trustees have any individual shares.

The legal ownership arrangement is matched by a new management scheme. There are two tiers. There is a partnership council which looks after the interests of the owners and an executive board that runs the company. The council consists of the three trustees and representatives of the partners. The chief executive is appointed by the trustees, but all other members of the executive board are appointed by the chief executive, with the consent of the trustees.

This is a scheme that sacrifices none of the advantages of a conventional free-enterprise company, yet has none of its disadvantages. Furthermore, the transfer can be made to partnership without an act of total self-sacrifice on the part of the original shareholders. Every worker in Baxi owns his or her job, and that is tremendously important. Labour is employing capital rather than vice versa. Short of a fundamental change in company law such as is advocated in the last section, this 'participation to partnership' transformation seems to go as far as is possible to meet the objections to existing UK law. Furthermore, it would seem to be a system that would be capable of continuing operation as the company grows organically. There would be a difficult problem should it prove necessary or desirable at some stage to merge with a conventional company.

## Nobody's Company

In 1951, when faced with a dilemma similar to Baxendale's, Ernest Bader chose a different constitution when divesting himself of the fruits of thirty years capital growth of the firm he founded, the Scott Bader Company Ltd. His solution was to set up a body – the Scott Bader Commonwealth – into which he vested total ownership of the firm. All his former employees, and all subsequent employees, became members of the Commonwealth, but nobody – including himself and members of his family – had a share in the capital of the Commonwealth. With the agreement of all members, a constitution was drawn up defining the ways in which powers and control would be distributed, and how profits would be handled. It contained several very radical features. A limit on its size was set in order to maintain a human scale, with the provision that, should further growth be desirable, it should be facilitated by setting up fully independent units on the same Commonwealth lines. To emphasize the nature of community fellowship in the Commonwealth, no member may be dismissed for any reason other than gross misconduct. Profit sharing had been practised by Bader prior to his divestment. After 60 per cent of net income has been allocated for taxation and ploughing back, 40 per cent is appropriated by the Commonwealth, half of which is distributed to members as pay-bonuses and the remainder allocated by members to agreed charitable purposes. In this way profit-sharing continues.

The Scott Bader experiment, which has performed satisfactorily for nearly forty years (though not without its share of crises and setbacks), has become a model for many more common-ownership small firms whose members share Bader's basic, self-denying ideal that nobody should gain capital wealth from the labours of others. The company board of directors is appointed by the members, and is accountable to them, so it has much in common with other forms of worker-cooperative. This is probably the main difference from the Baxi scheme. Many will argue that a worker-cooperative form of control can easily blunt the edge of management; often this is not in the best long-term interests of the enterprise. My own attempts to involve colleagues in difficult decisions have confirmed that there are those who are too often unwilling to be party to them. So I am inclined to prefer the Baxi system in which such decisions can be taken by an executive board in the long-term interests of the company. This particular point is of much less significance in small companies, and many common-ownership companies are small or very small.

I have concentrated, on the one hand, on a fundamental change in company law such as has been envisaged by George Goyder and, on the other, on two schemes that are in operation, which in their different ways seek to go as far as possible, within the existing legal system, to overcome the main objections to the conventional joint-stock limited liability system. I have not dealt with the various systems of co-determination that have evolved in recent years. They do have some effect on management, and they do recognize some rights of employees that were previously absent, but they do not answer the point that 'it is iniquitous to give control of an organisation, dependent on the daily cooperation of free men and women, to absentee landlords from now until doomsday.'[11]

So long as the basic injustice remains I believe that it will become increasingly difficult to manage businesses that no longer require a large, unskilled labour force but that, of necessity, have to be flexible and innovative whilst operating in a pluralistic business environment. A new generation of technology will be required to bring in the New Age. I believe it is rightly referred to as the second Industrial Revolution, and it covers the whole business spectrum. The need will not only be for 'tiny improvements in a thousand places', but for many radical changes in a million places.

The financial system that has evolved along with the joint-stock limited liability company has become increasingly averse to risk and short-term in outlook. So long as control remains with these absentee landlords, managers will be in a strait-jacket. Hardly any financial institution understands technology. In the words of Robert A. Frosch, a Vice-president of General Motors, their main contribution to the creative process is 'to tell you what you need to know won't pay'. If managers are to be enabled to manage in an environment of uncertainty in which they have to invent the future, they must not be restrained by owners who are averse to risk and interested only in short-term returns on their existing investments.

## Summary

In chapter 5 the need for managers and employees – the players in the orchestra – to have a real sense of ownership of their jobs was recognized as a prerequisite for the degree of commitment that is increasingly called for in the exciting but risky business of innovation. Not only is authoritarian management out of fashion; so also are big battalions of unskilled and semi-skilled workers. The highly skilled and professional people that are the business players of the future cannot be fully motivated in an organization that is dedicated solely to the benefit of absentee landlords – the equity shareholders. This is one very practical reason why corporate ownership is of importance in the management of sustainable development.

There are other equally practical reasons why the nature of ownership and the legal constitution are important:

1 The existing system promotes movement towards an increasing degree of concentration in fewer and bigger companies. With this system the optimum size of companies in different industrial and commercial sectors cannot be attained.
2 Present equity ownership emphasizes the short-term. It rejects the long-term investment perspective that is essential for sustainable development.
3 Innovative risk-taking, which is essential for the creation of a radically different 'conserver' economy, is discouraged by the

existence of slow-moving, excessively bureaucratic businesses that are preoccupied with obtaining rapid returns on investment.

4 The secretiveness that is engendered by the present system of ownership and constitution is contrary to the need for openness and the involvement of employees in the New Age.

The moral reason for changes in corporate ownership and constitution (referred to in the opening paragraph of this chapter) is most important because it is fundamental, but these other *practical* reasons for favouring the kind of alternative systems that have been outlined also have their place.

## Notes

\* R. H. Tawney, *Commonplace Book* for 8 January 1914.
 1 M. Thatcher. Address to the General Assembly of the United Nations, 8 November 1989.
 2 E. F. Schumacher, *Small is Beautiful*.
 3 P. Hill, *Towards a New Philosophy*.
 4 G. Goyder, *The Just Enterprise*.
 5 Lord Justice Evershed, quoted in G. Goyder, *The Just Enterprise*.
 6 C. Southgate, quoted in Clutterbuck and Crainer, *The Decline and Rise of British Industry*.
 7 G. Goyder, *The Just Enterprise*.
 8 C. Handy, *Understanding Organisations*. Penguin Business, 1985.
 9 G. Goyder, *The Just Enterprise*.
10 P. Baxendale, private communication.
11 G. Goyder, *The Just Enterprise*.

# 8

# Quality, Codes and Standards

Our [1980] cars had luxury, style, performance – and poor quality.

Sir John Egan, Chairman of Jaguar Cars

Eighty percent of quality problems are caused by management.

Philip Crosby, International Quality Consultant

It is absolutely essential that management is totally committed to quality; and that this commitment becomes, without any question in the minds of subordinates, a fundamental and unchanging part of their management style.

John Jennings, Shell Group Managing Director

The paradigm change of attitudes that is becoming evident as a result of the developing concerns described in chapter 1 requires that a new meaning is given to the concept of quality. To make this new meaning effective will require a critical review of codes of practice and standards that have evolved under the influence of the traditional meaning.

## Evolution of Quality Concepts

In the early part of the industrial age the business concept of quality applied to products, but not to the whole range of business activities. For example, a service was either satisfactory or unsatisfactory but the term 'quality service' was not common parlance. In so far as products were concerned, quality was mainly associated with expensive items. For a considerable time, and often with little justification, hand-made goods alone were considered to be quality products. It was some time before machine-made things produced in volume were recognized as being of a quality equal to hand-made equivalents.

The drive to achieve lower unit costs of production has been matched by a constant striving after improvements to meet the growing expectations of customers and market competitiveness. A visit to any industrial museum provides a striking illustration of a step-by-step advance – 'of tiny improvements in a thousand places'. In the past durability and repairability were generally considered to be crucial characteristics of quality products. They remain important in many products made for industrial or commercial use. Indeed for some products, such as jet engines for airline use, durability and repairability have improved enormously. Previously overhaul periods (with the replacement of parts) were every few hundred hours. Now these engines run perfectly, without extensive maintenance, for thousands of hours.

The same thing has not happened with consumer products. On the contrary, durability and repairability have in many cases been reduced under the influence of fashion marketing and the drive for high-volume production. Consequently the general public no longer considers these particular qualities to be as important as they once did.

It was the substitution of the concept of marketing for the traditional notion of business as the provider of the goods and services essential for the sustenance of a dignified life that fundamentally changed the concept of quality. If one takes, for example, the universal human need for self-respect, there is available a vast potential range of goods that may claim to meet it. Any single item in the range may have little intrinsic worth in terms of performance or of durability. An item of clothing may provide little warmth and may only survive for a few weeks; another may be thrown away because it cannot be cleaned. The quality of such products would be judged largely on aesthetic or fashion grounds, which are as changeable as the weather, or might be signalled by a so-called designer label. Such is the influence of the marketing concept on the meaning of quality.

## Quality Management

Although some new criteria have gained prominence, whilst some like durability or repairability have declined in importance, there are other very important dimensions in which the meaning of quality has expanded in business. First, quality is no longer only associated with the finished good or service. Quality is now perceived across the entire spectrum of business activity, so much so that it is now realistic to refer to a company as a 'quality company'. Such a firm is one in which the management and workpeople have an unqualified commitment to the achievement of excellence in all aspects of its life and activities. 'Total quality management' (TQM) is the label used with this most recent meaning of quality in business. In the last ten years it has become a world-wide movement. The importance attached to it is summed up by Hans Wrage, the Marketing Director of Deutsche Shell. He says 'quality is the key to success; it has to prevail in everything we do.' Some of the old myths about quality have been laid to rest. 'Quality is free' says Philip Crosby, a leading proponent of TQM. By this he means that quality operations produce a handsome profit, rather than add cost as was previously believed. Faults, errors and reworking in service companies not uncommonly account for something like 40 per cent of operating costs. In manufacturing companies scrap, reworking and other errors have amounted to a quarter of total costs. By following an approach of total quality management it is claimed that this costly waste can be cut to about 5 per cent.

The achievement of such an improvement not only requires a belief that quality is free; it also necessarily requires the humble acceptance by managers that they cause 80 per cent or more of quality problems. Instead of looking for scapegoats amongst employees, managers have to look for solutions in a climate of openness to prevent problems occurring. Another myth is that 'zero defects' is an impossible counsel of perfection. Provided all the detailed, essential requirements of the business are carefully and precisely defined, 'zero defects' is the *only* acceptable performance standard.

In chapter 2 I described how the detailed performance requirements of motor fuel were transformed from arbitrary technical specifications into clearly defined levels of customer satisfaction that had to be maintained at all times of the year for all vehicles. Another quality in marketing operations is the speed with which orders are satisfied. In one company I enquired about its delivery performance. I was told that there was no defined prescription for this important aspect of company activity. It was with some difficulty that I was able to obtain a picture from the order and despatch records. Only a small proportion of orders were being despatched within two days of receipt, and a shockingly high proportion were still outstanding after five. Within a few weeks of defining the required standard of prompt delivery and of introducing a suitable but simple monitoring system, a 'zero defects' performance was achieved. A similar 'quality management' approach to the delayed receipt of payment for goods delivered quickly reduced the financial losses that were being incurred. The company had been tolerating the situation as I found it; what appeared to many to be good enough was not at all good enough for the 'quality company' it aspired to be. It was only when it became possible to calculate the benefits and costs of the rapid delivery of goods and the prompt settlement of invoices that everyone could see that poor quality cost more than high-quality.

## Developing a Quality Culture

Quality management cannot be successful in a traditional, hierarchical kind of operation. It requires the understanding and enthusiastic, active involvement of every employee and a tireless commitment at all levels of management. A quality culture, once created, has to be sustained; and resources have to be provided to cover essential costs. In all matters of quality nothing is free, but the returns on investment are very high. The importance attached to this expanded concept of quality is well illustrated by the setting up, by the French Chamber of Commerce and Industry in cooperation with employers organizations, of a national network for promoting total quality.

The quality culture has to be instilled through effective training and two-way communication. The best vehicle is a form of 'action learning' in organized small groups dealing with everyday matters in great detail. The traditional philosophy of quality control was to prevent faulty goods reaching customers by means of thorough inspection. The new approach is preventive. It aims to get things right first time, every time. Thereby it minimizes the need for inspection. The task of a quality working group is to identify the cause of a quality problem and to propose a solution that will prevent any occurrence or reoccurrence of a fault. To do the job, every member of the group needs to be able to use techniques which hitherto have been considered the preserve of 'quality specialists' – bar charting, statistical process control, cause and effect diagrams etc. With quality management everyone in the team is responsible. No longer is quality the sole responsibility of professionals. Consequently quality management is a powerful force for the development of a participative, innovative enterprise.

## A New Meaning of Quality

It might be thought that TQM is the last word in quality matters. It might have been had change been continuous. But with changes that are now *discontinuous*, that are expected to produce a radical transformation in business life, quality will have a new significance, and it will have added dimensions that have not been traditionally seen as part of a quality operation.

We are beginning to see evidence of this in the food industry. A quality milk is not only one that has come from a particular breed of tuberculin-tested cow; it now has to be the product of a tested cow that has not been treated with bovine somatrophin hormone (BST), that has fed only on grass and organic cake. Similar qualifications are made for other foodstuffs, with claims that they are uncontaminated, natural products which are free from additives and unnatural treatments such as irradiation. For most of my career in product development additives were considered to be beneficial. Even lead anti-knock additives were considered to be a mark of quality in the 1930s; now lead-free fuel is preferred. It is not only that purity has been added to the list of desirable quality characteristics. The whole process of production is reinstated as an element of quality. For example, free range eggs are considered superior to factory-farm eggs.

Paper is another product whose process of production is becoming a quality factor. At one time recycled paper was considered to be inferior; now it has acquired a connotation of quality because of concerns about the environment and natural resources that are beginning to influence customers' choices. As time passes they are likely to become a dominant factor. Already processes are becoming sophisticated. The traditional bleaching process used in the manufacture of paper results in toxic substances that pollute the environment. A paper mill of average size discharges 50 tonnes of chlorinated chemicals every day. One is the highly poisonous dioxin. It is very soluble in fats and is 70,000 times as deadly as cyanide in some mammals. As a result of public concern about the effects of dioxin and other chlorinated chemicals on humans, an alternative process is coming into favour in which hydrogen peroxide is the bleaching agent. Consequently 'chlorine free' is a quality mark to be added to recycled paper. No longer can the public be satisfied with a dirty industrial system that results in the need for additional effort and expenditure to clean up the mess. There is a growing public demand for basically clean technologies as a more rational approach to the reduction of waste and environmental conservation. This is certain to make processes of production increasingly a new factor of quality.

There was a time when the cutlery label 'Made in Sheffield' was understood to signify high quality. The location of production has similarly denoted quality for some other products, such as Waterford crystal, Scotch whisky and Devonshire cream. As the making of many common products, such as cutlery, spread geographically, some of the influence of the place of production as a mark of quality decreased. However, as the manufacture of many consumer items disperses into small, local units, it may be expected that 'locally made' will gain strength as a mark of excellence. There is a recent example in the Isle of Purbeck. A local farmer has diversified into the manufacture of ice-cream and has chosen to promote his product as Purbeck Ice Cream. In time we may see 'Made in Wareham' on a pullover label or 'Made in Swanage' on a pair of trousers.

Probably the most important new meaning of quality in consumer goods will be durability and repairability, with energy efficiency applying to domestic equipment. It has already begun to appear in the promotion of some makes of car, starting with extended rust-free guarantees. This was originally based on such things as the sealing of the underbody and cavity wax treatments. The incorporation of galvanized steel in some models has been the next claim.

Repairability has not yet featured significantly as a quality characteristic of consumer goods, though it is an important consideration in the choice of industrial plant and for products used in commerce. With energy efficiency, the importance of repairability will spread once the economic and environmental advantage of extended useful life becomes recognized. In the long run the contribution that both durability and repairability can make to a less wasteful use of scarce and increasingly expensive materials will be valued.

Thus, with this new meaning of quality, a product or service will come to be seen as good not only because of its intrinsic worth to the user, but also because in every respect it contributes to a sustainable way of life. To be of good quality it must not only satisfy all the traditional needs of individuals, but must also contribute positively to the general well-being through the sparing use of resource, appropriate technology and environmental harmony.

## Standards

It is very probable that changes in the meaning of quality will have a big influence on the future development of technical standards. To some managers this may be disappointing. It is very understandable that anyone who has had to wrestle with the difficulties of meeting a wide variety of national or customer specifications might take a jaundiced view of the whole subject. The thought that additional criteria, such as efficiency in the use of energy, durability and repairability, may soon be added may not be at all welcome.

Fortunately there is a compensating factor, and it is of particular relevance to European companies. One of the most helpful aspects of the development of a single European market is the harmonization of the various national systems of technical standards applying to industry and commerce. To anyone who has tried to do business across national boundaries it will be no surprise to learn that it has been estimated that £130 billion would be saved were historic barriers to be removed; and that divergent national technical standards were the second most costly item after bureaucratic formalities and border controls.[1] Across the EEC countries alone, 100,000 different technical specification items were identified. For companies marketing across the world, the existence of this plethora of different standards in the domestic European market is intolerable. The creation of a common EEC system of harmonized standards will be a major improvement from which most European companies will benefit.

However, there will remain the special standards that individual customers make. Most are reasonable and well justified. These can give no cause for complaint. However, some are neither reasonable nor well founded. They often reflect the eccentric view of a technical specialist. I recall being asked to supply a protective product to a large customer whose specification was deficient. The offer of a well-proven, internationally marketed, protective compound was rejected by the customer's purchasing department and discussion with the technical quality control manager was fruitless. The order was eventually fulfilled according to the customer's requirements, but several months later a claim was received complaining that the product did not give adequate protection!

The harmonization process of European national standards is one that needs to be followed by managers. These standards have been an important tool by means of which some countries have successfully protected themselves from foreign competition. However, the task of breaking down these old trade barriers is not an easy one. It can be assisted through the cooperation of managers who have experienced frustration from them.

## New European Standards Institutes

The prospects for fairly rapid progress have been much improved since the old, time-consuming and bureaucratic harmonization approach was replaced by a new, multidimensional strategy. The breakthrough came with the Internal Market White Paper in which the Commissioner, Lord Cockfield, called for an important distinction, in all internal market legislation, between what is essential to harmonize, and what may be left to mutual recognition of national standards. Harmonization of essential technical legislation will be restricted to areas such as minimum health and safety requirements. The principle of qualified majority voting in the Council of Ministers, under an amended treaty, will greatly facilitate approval. Conformity with these limited minimum standards, which apply only where it is vital to create a uniform European market, will guarantee right of access to all the markets of community members. Non-essential national standards will be mutually recognized on the assumption that, if a product is lawfully manufactured and marketed in one member state, there is no valid reason why it should not be acceptable to all other community members. Three standards institutes – the European Committee for Standardisation (CEN), the European Telecommunications Standards Institute (ETSI) and the European Committee for Electrotechnical Standards (CENELEC) – are authorized by the commission to develop standards for industrial products throughout the Community. The testing of products and certification procedures are also subject to the same principle of mutual recognition. A new body – EUROCERT – has been created. It is composed of member states' inspection and certification organizations. Its job is to ensure that product certificates issued by one member will be easily accepted by all others.

Compliance with national or international standards will play an important part in the development of globally sustainable economies, and in the stabilization of environmental and ecological systems. International industry and trade organizations, such as the International Chamber of Commerce and the various European manufacturers federations, have demonstrated leadership in dealing with environmental issues. They will be in a good position to take a lead in handling the extended, integrated concerns of sustainable economic development. However, in the past such bodies have tended to be dominated by the interests of large companies. With the revived and growing importance of small and medium-sized firms all over the world, it is necessary that they should be equally represented in determining standards in all industries.

If there is to be a sufficient rate of progress towards the sustainable development described in the report of the World Commission on Environment and Development,[2] the response of industry and commerce must not be limited to mere compliance with minimum national or international standards and regulations. A greater sense of responsibility on the part of company boards, managements, trade unions and employees is necessary. There needs to be a serious commitment to company strategies and policies that are, as far as possible, in advance of official standards with the object of raising general standards progressively. Small and medium-sized firms should not be excluded. Their contribution should be in the form of strategies that are appropriate for their size.

## Codes of Practice

Standards of relevant quality characteristics that advance regularly can play a vital part in the development of a society whose use of resources and environmental improvement is sustainable into the future. However, their role is a limited one. They can do no more than exclude from the market those products whose quality is unacceptably poor. If there is to be general, rapid progress in the efficient use of resources, the reduction of unnecessary waste, the preservation of animal and plant species and the quality of air, soil and water, these minimum standards must not be allowed to detract from the development in companies of quality cultures that strive to reach ever higher levels of achievement. To assist them in promoting quality cultures managers need clear vision and shared values for their companies; these are obtained through training and supportive codes of good practice.

Prototype codes have been in existence for some years. The one published by the British Institute of Management is a good example.[3] Mostly they were evolved out of experience gained in the period preceding the present paradigm change; however, the most recent printings incorporate guidelines that reflect the growing concern with the environment, natural resources and society. As new experience is gained in the innovative management of uncertainty, company codes will need to be reviewed and brought up to date, perhaps, at five-year intervals.

---

**Box 2** *As Regards the Environment, Natural Resources and Society*

The Professional Manager should:

- Recognise his organisation's obligations to its owners, employees, suppliers, customers, users, society and the environment;
- Make the most effective use of all natural resources and energy sources for the benefit of the organisation and with minimum detriment to the public interest;
- Avoid harmful pollution, and wherever economically possible, reprocess or recycle waste material;
- Ensure that all public communications are true and not misleading;
- Be willing to exercise his influence and skill for the benefit of society within which he and his organisation operate.[4]

---

Much necessary innovation will have a high technological content. It will be important that codes of good engineering and technological practice should be available to guide engineers and technologists. No longer can financial considerations be allowed to interfere in matters that could affect sustainability, any more than they have been allowed to influence matters of safety. Since technological considerations of sustainability may from time to time conflict with financial considerations, it is essential that managers' codes should be in harmony with those of their professional colleagues.

## Impact of Sustainable Development

The widespread commitment of national governments throughout Europe to a form of development that is sustainable in the long term has many significant implications for engineers and technologists, as well for company boards and managers. For example, the minimum first cost of durable goods can no longer be an adequate, single objective. A greater concern must be the 'whole-life' cost of the article in both financial and non-financial measures. 'Whole-life' cost cannot be evaluated simply in terms of the direct costs incurred in production, distribution and use. Every economic activity occurs within the context of a society. In many instances there are costs which, till now, have not been borne by those directly concerned, but instead by society and the environment. As the concept of 'the polluter pays' is enforced, these hitherto externalized costs will have to become part of the evaluation of 'whole-life' cost. They will not be confined to environmental pollution. For instance, in the case of motor cars there are considerable costs associated with the provision of roads and traffic management, which increase greatly as the car population grows. Not all costs can be measured satisfactorily in financial terms. It sometimes seems as though an object can only exist when a financial value is placed on it. Road accidents certainly have associated financial costs, but they also have non-financial costs which are very often the most important.

This all points to a fundamental change in the way that technological and engineering development is tackled. The traditional approach has been to concentrate attention on particular, detailed improvements in a product or process to the exclusion of everything else. For example, an immense amount of technical ingenuity, effort and money has been devoted for decades to the improvement of the design of steam-turbine blades. As a result there have been very worthwhile increases in the efficiency with which electricity is generated. Despite the fact that far greater losses were being incurred than could ever be gained through improvements in generating efficiency, comparatively little attention was given to the recovery and use of the wasted heat that was a by-product of the system. Our perception has been narrow. Electricity was the only thing that concerned us and we aimed to generate it with maximum efficiency at minimum cost. This might be described as a 'blinkered approach' to technical development, in which little or no attention has been paid to any other aspects of our activity than the central concern. Such an approach did not only exist in power generation: it was prevalent in almost all fields of technological development.

## A 'Total Systems Approach'

If we are to cope successfully with the challenge that long-term sustainable development presents, we shall have to abandon that 'blinkered approach' and replace it with a 'total systems approach'. Equal importance will have to be given to all the waste and other side-effects that are created in the production, distribution and use of products – including the ultimate disposal of production plants. Where mass-produced products are concerned, early attention will have to be given to side-effects that only create problems when the products are in mass use.

A 'total systems approach' applies to processes as well as to products. I am indebted to Professor T. D. Patten for drawing my attention to an interesting example in the oil industry. Crude oil arriving at a well-head in the North Sea carries with it associated gases, sand and water from the underground reservoir. These are separated from the crude oil and the water is discharged into the sea. When water is injected into the reservoir to maintain the reservoir pressure, increasing quantities of water are entrained. In time the quantity of water that is passed through the separation plant can become greater than the quantity of oil produced. The 'blinkered approach' to plant design would focus on crude oil from which contaminants have to be removed. A 'total systems approach', on the other hand, would give equal attention to the production of water of a quality that is acceptable for discharge into the sea. It is quite likely that a designer briefed to produce a plant in which one of the principal products was uncontaminated water would produce some-thing different from one that had just crude oil as its main product.

If the main objective of a building design is to provide accommodation requiring the minimum consumption of energy, a 'total systems approach' will visualize a building very different from one conceived with a 'blinkered approach'; the latter will produce a building that requires 'bolt-on' systems to heat and light it and that will be profligate in the use of energy.

An important element in future codes of good practice – for all professionals, managers and employees – will be the adoption of a 'total systems approach' in place of the traditional 'blinkered approach'.

## Humanizing Technologies

In view of the necessity to make the best use of the human factor in innovative businesses, it is important for engineers and technologists to ensure that production processes enhance the unique human skills and knowledge of employees and managers. It has been said that work should make people think and enjoy. The 'blinkered approach' in the past has frequently taken little or no account of the human factor, and its exclusion means that we are often far from optmizing the whole system. A striking example of loss resulting from such neglect was referred to by Frederick Herzberg in his book *Work and the Nature of Man*. He wrote of '. . . a job that required the mentality and motivation of a child. Argyris demonstrated this by bringing in mentally retarded patients to do an extremely routine job in a factory setting. He was rewarded by the patients increasing production by 400%.' Codes for managers and professionals need to incorporate the challenge to install production systems that make the best use of the partnership between human beings and plant.

---

**Box 3** *Outline Code of Engineering for Sustainable Development*

- The primary purpose of civil applications of engineering is to harness the forces and resources of nature for the benefit of mankind and the environment, in both the long and short term.
- In order that the benefits may be as widely available as possible, it is essential that:
  1. natural resources should be used as efficiently as possible, and that renewable resources are preferred;
  2. the financial cost to the users of the product, over its whole life, should be as low as possible;

---

3 the product should not demand exceptional skill from its users;

4 the processes of production and of use should be designed in such a way that the people involved are not dehumanized.

- The highest possible technical standards of durability, repairability and, where appropriate, energy efficiency, should be aimed at.

- An engineering project's short- and long-term effects on mankind and the environment must be considered in any evaluation of its benefits and costs.

- Every undertaking must respect human rights and cherish human dignity. Engineering should not be carried out with the intention of giving some people advantages at the expense of others. In so far as any sectional advantage may be unavoidable, engineering should give it to the disadvantaged.

- When designing a product or a process a 'total systems approach' should be adopted. Products should be designed and manufactured in such a way that maintenance, repair and reconditioning are made easy; the materials of construction should be recyclable whenever possible.

- Due consideration should be given to the potential for misuse, and appropriate measures should be taken to prevent it.

- Ultimate disposal of a product of engineering work, at the end of its useful life, must be considered at the design stage, and plans for acceptable solutions prepared.

- Knowledge regarding safety, for people and the natural environment, should be freely shared.

- No relevant information regarding the use and application of a product should be withheld.

- Respect must be paid to all patented inventions and registered designs.

- Involvement in the design, development and production of illegal goods is forbidden.

## Shifting Values

Earlier in this chapter the reinstatement of durability as a quality factor was discussed. I suggest that it is unlikely to become a major advertising claim unless there is a change in market values.

Traditionally, in their innovative role, businesses have been very effective in modifying market values. Their ability to change minds from the satisfaction of necessities to the development of wants has been central to the marketing revolution of the last fifty years. When Peter Drucker wrote 'the purpose of a business is to create a customer' he was describing a fundamental shift in market values.

That particular transformation fitted perfectly the main economic development philosophy of the time. The indiscriminate growth of financial transactions, nationally and globally, was the single objective. The emergence of a different single aim – sustainable development – has made the Drucker definition obsolete. Businesses must change accordingly, because this is not an arbitrary change of objective. It is a change that is forced upon us by all the demands of the planet, with which there can be no compromise. The growth of financial transactions can no longer be indiscriminate. They must be made to conform to the conditions dictated by the planet for sustainability.

## From a 'Consumer' to a 'Conserver' Economy

Just as the revolution in marketing depended upon the success of businesses in producing a fundamental shift in market values, so, as we move into the New Age of sustainable development, businesses will have to bring about another shift that is in tune with the new situation. So far in the present transition, most of the initiative has not been coming from businesses. Pressure groups such as Friends of the Earth and Greenpeace have influenced the market. Businesses, sometimes reluctantly, have been dragged along by that influence. To be successful a business needs to be swimming strongly *with* the stream, not being dragged along *by* it. An innovative business will always be at the vanguard of progress, inventing the future. To be successful a business needs to move enthusiastically with the market. Unfortunately the movement has sometimes been decidedly unenthusiastic! It is for this reason that the most important change in codes of good practice for managers and professionals is the addition of clauses that call for a commitment to initiatives that are in harmony with long-term, sustainable global development. A factor in the implementation of such a commitment will be the incorporation of constraints in national and international standards that will ensure that all development is compatible. The necessary shift in values is

> To produce more of what you want whilst using less of what you have is basic to the teaching of all engineers. It is part of our fundamental philosophy.
>
> *Robert Malpas CBE, F.Eng. Chairman of POWERGEN*[5]

now fundamental. We require a movement from a 'consumer' economy to a 'conserver' economy.

To emphasize the importance of common standards as facilitators of good practice, I can quote two cases from personal experience that have been frustrated as a result of their absence. Twenty years ago I patented a method for the prevention of exhaust smoke from diesel engines. It has not been possible to make it commercial because no common standard exists that requires diesel engines to be self-controlled with respect to their exhaust smoke emissions. Another potentially important device prevents anyone who has been drinking above the legal limit from starting a car engine. There is little prospect for the sale of such a device on the free market in the absence of a common standard requiring that a car engine should be designed so that it cannot be started by a person who has been drinking in excess of the limit.

## Environmental Audit Systems Needed

Something more will be needed to complement new standards, new codes and a new meaning of quality. Systems for environmental internal audit will be required so that managers and employees can see the degree of success or failure that is being achieved as a result of the policies that have been adopted. Internal audit systems will also confirm compliance with official laws and regulations. The International Chamber of Commerce has published a useful guide on environmental auditing.[6] As well as giving detailed suggestions for the auditing process, it points out that it can have beneficial side effects. Matters needing attention are identified, giving timely warnings so that potential problems may be avoided. Relations with the authorities and the public can be helped on a basis of greater mutual confidence. Sometimes even cost savings can be made when avoidable waste is identified.

# Summary

The contemporary spread of the practice of total quality management and the intensive development of harmonized European standards provide a unique opportunity for the effective implementation of the new meaning of quality that sustainable development requires.

A set of standards for sustainability will play a very important part in any change of economic direction. However, minimum quality levels will have to be raised regularly as technical capability increases. Codes of good practice for managers and for business professionals will be needed to provide the necessary dynamic for such development. To ensure that everything possible is being done, every company needs to have an annual environmental audit.

## Notes

1 *The European Challenge 1992: the Benefits of a Single Market*, a report. EEC.
2 *Our Common Future*, a report. World Commission on Environment and Development, Oxford University Press, 1987.
3 *Code of Conduct and Guides to Good Management Practice*. British Institute of Management, 1984.
4 Ibid.
5 R. Malpas, Global Forces towards Greater Energy Efficiency. A lecture to the Fellowship of Engineering, London, 1989.
6 *Environmental Auditing*. International Chamber of Commerce, 1988.

# 9

# New Rules for the Business Game

Better to change before we are changed.

John Harvey-Jones*

All that has been discussed earlier , other than in chapter 7, has been about direct action within companies by managers at all levels. But every company operates within a particular social, cultural and political environment. What managers are able to achieve as leaders depends to a large extent on the attitudes and morale of the employees and the communities in which they operate. Achievement also depends on the rules of the business game that have evolved over decades through the influence of the underlying beliefs and assumptions of the past. It is quite possible to progress some way towards sustainable development under the old rules. But the remainder of the journey cannot be travelled without considerable changes in those rules and the habits of thought and action of people in business.

Of course, it is true that change will be less disruptive if we move in advance, changing direction deliberately in the way that appears right. But where radical change is required, *we* have to be changed before effective action can follow.

This book is about the transformation of management: its main obstacle is habit. The habits of management that need to be overcome are those that have developed over many years as a by-product of the old visions and values of industry and commerce. They are deeply ingrained, and they will not be quickly and easily overcome.

## Changing Habits of Thought and Action

To start the transformation in a company there has to be a total commitment by the board and senior managers to a new vision and new values that will create enthusiasm and capture the imagination of the whole work-force; they must also be in tune with sustainable economic development. Often when attempts are made to introduce new schemes, for example quality circles, this necessary preliminary is forgotten. A gardening metaphor is appropriate: new seed cannot be expected to germinate and grow unless the ground has been thoroughly prepared. Before any attempt is made to do anything to break old habits, it is essential for the gardening work to be completed; otherwise the entire project will be counter-productive. When I was responsible for the provision of training programmes for some of our marketing people, the exercise for some trainees was doomed to failure from the start because their senior managers had not shown why the training was needed and how it fitted in with the company's policies. Only when widespread understanding and enthusiasm for the new vision and values have been achieved should the next step be taken.

The second stage of transformation is an integrated and comprehensive programme of management training and development. It must cover all levels of management; its purpose will be to inculcate styles and practices that are appropriate to the new ways in which the company will operate as a result of changes in vision and values. The matters covered in chapters 5–8 are particularly relevant. The entire company will need to become a learning organization. Although there will need to be some class-room work, most will be done through 'action learning'. Such a transformation project cannot hope to succeed if it is just superimposed on an organization that is already stretched to the limit with its day to day work. Steps must be taken in advance to make room for it, either by increasing capacity or by lightening the load. Furthermore, the project will fail unless senior managers remain fully involved from its beginning to its end. The process of changing the habits of a lifetime is a difficult and painful one for many people. Any sign that senior managers may have withdrawn to do other, 'more important' things is likely to cause the project to fail. Regular reviews of progress are essential.

The demands of such a transformation programme will probably seem fantastic to many readers. They should not be deceived into believing that they can, in the long run, be avoided. The only choice is whether to do it calmly on one's own initiative, or to be forced into it by external circumstances in some future crisis.

## Retaining Control when Power is Devolved

One of the main problems facing managements of traditional, hierarchically organized, large companies is the retention of proper control as they move to much more decentralized operations. Schumacher drew attention to the 'principle of subsidiarity', whose origin is Catholic social philosophy. A papal encyclical states

It is an injustice, a grave evil and a disturbance of right order to assign to a greater and higher association what lesser and subordinate organisations can do. For every social activity ought of its very nature to furnish help to the members of the body social and never destroy or absorb them.[1]

So much that is amiss with large, bureaucratic and unwieldy businesses is so because they do not conform to that principle. But it is important that lower levels – whether subsidiary companies, divisions, departments or sections – are given the authority and resources that are commensurate with their capacity and competence. Having been given the greatest authority possible, managers need to be told what must be authorized at a higher level after consideration in a wider context. When managers at all levels are convinced that this is the principle upon which the whole organization operates, nobody need fear that control has been lost as powers of decision are devolved. So it is important to make the commitment to this principle explicit throughout the whole business organization.

A major and fundamental change took place in the Shell Group in 1959. Previously much of its operation had been centralized in the London and Hague head offices. When the change came, the title of manager was abolished in these offices and the major groupings were called coordinations. As an illustration of the degree of devolution that took place, the marketing coordinator retained only one overriding power: that concerned the integrity of the Shell emblem and colour scheme. At the time the change occurred, the principle governing the allocation of authority in the new organization was not explained clearly enough at all levels. I believe that the amount of unease that persisted amongst many members of the staff for a long time would have been less, and of shorter duration, if the principle had been widely proclaimed and understood.

## Flexible and Responsive Management Information

Many existing information systems are too systematic and rigid to be suitable for very innovative and rapidly changing operation. They frequently do little more than assist in monitoring and control. In so far as they help with the planning process they are seldom capable of contributing anything more than is required for a continuation of the existing business. They may be good administratively, but they lack something that is needed for innovative management. The system that is needed should be capable of alerting managers to new or unused opportunities, and to any danger that lies ahead. By linking information on dangers or opportunities with other data, creative ideas will be initiated that will enable the dangers to be avoided or the opportunities seized.

The information about monitoring, control and conventional business planning is mostly made available in numerical form – as totals, percentages, ratios etc. These are useful mathematical abstractions which, if used carefully and with understanding, are very valuable for certain purposes. But they are not the 'real world'. The kind of information required for creative thinking may sometimes be quantitative, but mostly it will be an association of practical observations. With the greatly increased capacity of computers to store, analyse and relate information, they should be able to help facilitate the generation of creative ideas and initiatives.

## Making Team Decisions Effective

As we move from the age of hierarchical, top-down decision-making into an age of team consent, there is an obstacle that must be overcome if the proposed transformation is to be effective. Any rearrangement of work will reveal that there are some people who can sense personal advantage and others who feel that they are threatened. When the decision-making process involves all employees, there is likely to be considerable resistance to change unless the future interests of those who are likely to feel threatened receive at least as much attention and sympathy as their colleagues. Obviously the measures that can be taken will vary from company to company. However, if the future general pattern of working arrangements is seen to be more pluralistic (as was described in chapter 5, involving more small firms and self-employment), a carefully planned programme to develop independent enterprise, designed to use the talents of redundant employees, should form an integral part of reorganization.

Whilst I was involved with the development of local enterprise trusts several of the large companies I was working with, that were undergoing major changes, successfully explored the matching of surplus resources with the skills and abilities of some of their employees for whom they could see no continuing employment in their companies. Another approach was to see what services were being imported from outside the local community that might with advantage be provided locally if a new enterprise was set up. (There are many examples, such as the one mentioned earlier of Xerox employees being helped to work from home with the freedom to take work from other companies as well as from their previous employers.) The shift towards more durable, high-quality products, combined with an expansion of maintenance, repair and reconditioning, will provide another very attractive range of opportunities for people who were previously employed in production. Such people will carry with them invaluable knowledge and skills to apply to their new employment.

## The Financial Environment of Small Firms and Cooperatives

Finance is an area in which small firms face special problems. This particularly affects those that are young and have not reached full stability and maturity. As financial institutions grow, and global money-markets seem to have no better reason for existence than to provide opportunities for financiers to make money out of money, the investment needs of industry in general, and small firms in particular, have been largely ignored. In contrast with the huge risks taken in loans to Third World countries the financial world has been extraordinarily unwilling to take risks in young businesses and has been obsessed with short-term returns and repayment. The situation varies considerably in the different countries of Europe. It is probably worst in the UK, where for most small firms there is little or no finance available from local sources. Risk-free property investments, which have provided very good opportunities for growth, attract investment in preference to risky industry and commerce.

## New Local Sources of Finance for Small Firms

Some examples from the United States illustrate the new local sources of finance for small businesses that will be required increasingly in Europe if the obstacles are to be overcome. Chicago, through its Association of Development Organizations (CANDO), makes loans available from neighbourhood lending programmes. Other examples are agencies with loan funds dedicated to special interest groups; a Women's Self Employment Project is one. It has followed the example of the Bangladeshi Grameen Bank, which uses 'peer group credit circles' to develop pressure within peer groups in lieu of collateral. Each circle has five female members. Together they decide which two members should receive the first loans. Only when those two loans have been repaid does the second pair become eligible for loans – and the fifth has to wait until those loans are repaid.

As a result of the development of large, centralized financial institutions in the UK almost all of an individual's money is beyond personal control. There is very little choice over what savings are used for. We have become so used to this deprivation that we are now largely unaware of it. Unless a variety of independent systems and schemes are introduced to restore some choice, small businesses will continue to lack badly needed risk finance.

## Local Currencies for Unconventional Trading

There are interesting examples from the past that may provide models for the future. One came into being in Guernsey in 1815, following the Napoleonic Wars. As a result of the wars the island was economically very hard hit, and recovery was prevented because of the heavy interest payments being made to creditors. (It was a situation similar to that experienced in many countries of the Third World nearly two hundred years later.) By the very simple measure of creating £4,000 of Guernsey State interest-free notes, the wealth process of wealth creation was restarted. Over a period of about 20 years, Guernsey evolved from a depression to real prosperity because further issues of notes were carefully controlled to avoid inflation.

In 1929 a similar initiative was made by the Burgomaster of Worgl in Austria. It also transformed an area very quickly, at a time when the Austrian national economy was in a lot of trouble. Unfortunately, the Austrian National Bank ultimately succeeded in prohibiting this initiative using local currency. By contrast, the Guernsey community currency is still intact because of the respect of British governments for the islanders' independence.

There are contemporary examples of local currency in British Columbia. One began on Vancouver Island in 1976 and has spread to the city of Vancouver. It is now called the Local Exchange Trading System. It uses what it calls a 'green dollar', which is equivalent in value to a Canadian dollar. Members of the system usually trade with each other in green dollars although, if they wish, debts may be paid off in Canadian dollars. Records are kept on computers, and transactions are subject to tax. The system is based on the following very simple and just principle – 'I have received 50 green dollars worth from Bill, and I promise to contribute that much to others. Bill, in turn, will be entitled to receive 50 green dollars worth from the members of the system.'

## Cooperatives' Special Finance Problems

Small cooperative firms are already a significant part of the population of small businesses in Europe, and they are growing in numbers. They frequently have even greater difficulties with loans than do other owner-managed firms.

In Britain, Industrial Common Ownership Finance (ICOF) was started in 1973 to meet a demand for start-up and expansion capital through a revolving loan fund. In 1987 an ICOF share issue of £500,000 for lending to cooperatives was oversubscribed; and in 1989 an Ethical Savings Account has been opened in association with the Co-operative Bank. Loans will be made to cooperatives from this account with ICOF's close supervision. This account is providing an attractive interest-bearing investment for individuals who wish to place money on deposit for the specific use of cooperatives. It is a useful illustration of what might be done by local organizations to provide finance for local commercial purposes, using the facilities of the existing banking system. If decentralization is to develop, that being a basic aspect of the paradigm change envisaged, it will be dependent upon a regaining of control over the use of money for the purpose of creating local wealth.

## Changing the Rules of the Game

In discussing the obstacles in the foregoing paragraphs we have not taken account of any change in the legal structure. To a considerable extent they have been obstacles that could be addressed directly by managers. The existing systems of commercial legislation have evolved gradually over many years under the influence of the kinds of perception and attitude that have ruled past economic development. A dominant belief has been that progress was dependent on more monetary transactions, and on an increase in the share of industry and commerce being provided through large companies. The systems of legislation, which have primarily been designed with them in mind, have reflected that belief. They have been largely inappropriate for small businesses and have worked against the interests of the small-business sector. In order that the development of a better balance of large, medium-sized and small companies may occur unhindered, there will need to be a reshaping of some legislation. Since it is in the long-term interests of all businesses that the mixture of sizes should be the best possible, managers from all types and sizes of business can play a useful and creative part in ensuring that the legislation changes made are the most effective in redressing the balance.

### Taxation for Sustainability

As we contemplate the changing pattern of industrial and commercial development, the increase in service activities, most of which are labour intensive with only modest levels of capital investment, is one of the most outstanding features. Goods that are more durable and consequently fewer in number are likely to be produced in ways that are even more capital intensive. With environmental considerations requiring conservation of both materials and energy, it would be helpful if capital-intensive production were heavily taxed. To help contain the greenhouse effect there is talk of a 'carbon tax'.

   The present mixture of taxation places a heavy burden on personal income. Past thinking has treated capital lightly – thereby encouraging investment in capital-intensive methods – and has taxed labour heavily. Heavy taxation of labour has contributed to the decline of labour-intensive maintenance and repair services. In order to reverse the process – discourage production and consumption of goods and encourage maintenance, repair, reconditioning, reuse and recycling – the balance of taxation will need to be changed. We will have to consider, for example, different rates of VAT for recycled materials and virgin materials, and for the purchase of goods and the purchase of services. The need to penalize pollution and other forms of environmental damage may provide alternative sources of government revenue such as 'carbon tax'. Conversely, subsidies may be a desirable way of influencing developments in ways that bring long-term benefits, by encouraging desirable practices like the growing of 'energy crops' (e.g. coppicing) or the recovery of waste. In 1982 Samuel Brittan wrote 'At the same time that labour has been heavily taxed, capital has been quite ridiculously subsidised'.[2] Correcting that asymmetry is just one of many changes in taxation and subsidy that will be needed.

## Quantity Discounts Restraint

One significant consequence of the growth of large national and international companies, particularly businesses previously served by small firms, has been the development of the very big volume discounts demanded by their powerful buyers. Economies of scale has been the excuse for negotiating such privileged terms. I know, both to my cost as a small-firm supplier and to my advantage as a large-company buyer, that such justification has been grossly exaggerated. A discount of more than 5 per cent based on economies of scale can rarely reflect reality, and there can be no justification for such discounts over 15 per cent.

It is argued that no companies are forced to make such offers, but that they do so to compete with others that make big volume discounts part of their pricing policy. However, the result of this practice is to distort the balance between large and small companies in the same business. Take, for example, the bakery trade. The cost of flour and other purchased goods and services constitutes a large part of the selling prices of the baker's products, so a large discount on those costs gives the big company a considerable advantage. Since the supplier of flour, for example, needs to arrange prices in order to generate enough sales, the difference in the price paid by large and small customers is a measure of how much David is subsidizing Goliath.

Many large companies' accounts show net profits of less than 10 per cent of sales revenue – most are about 5 per cent. Should such a company have typical costs of purchases between 50 and 70 per cent of sales revenue, a 20 per cent discount on the total cost of purchases is likely to be equivalent to more than the net profit of the company. In this sense it can be said that many large companies depend on their big discounts to remain profitable, and that many small firms are forced to charge somewhat higher prices for their products because they pay more for their supplies. If this distortion is to be corrected, and a natural balance between large and small companies achieved, legislation will be required to limit the effect of what is sometimes described as purchasing muscle by restricting supply discounts to a maximum of about 5%.

## Commercial Cannibalism: Control of Predators

It is not only the weak operation of legislation for fair trading that has given advantage to large companies. Positive steps taken to rationalize industries, in the false belief that bigger necessarily means more efficient, have played a part in the process of concentration. So too has the absence of effective legislation aimed at preventing any company take-over that will reduce competition. Throughout this century, in the absence of such legislation, and with a Monopolies and Mergers Commission that has very limited terms of reference and influence in matters concerning the acquisition of small and medium-sized firms, a large number of small British firms were taken over by large, predatory companies. In recent years the practice spread, with large companies themselves becoming victims. The latest feature in the history of commercial cannibalism is the appearance of operators who are making fortunes with 'junk bonds' by breaking up conglomerates.

Had the process of concentration been of universal benefit, producing more success for the merged or acquired companies, the case for restricting such activities would be weak. Unfortunately, in the last few decades, few firms involved in mergers or take-overs benefited; many declined and some totally failed. There can be no acceptable balance between the various sizes of industrial and commercial enterprise if this law of the jungle is allowed to continue. An outlawing of mergers or acquisition would be absurd and damaging; but a sensitive and selective legislative mechanism that involves managers and employees as well as shareholders is something that requires urgent attention.

Regulation needs to be tailored for companies of different sizes. Over the past hundred years a huge amount of regulation has been introduced as companies have grown in size; and more can be expected particularly in matters of environmental and consumer protection. All this regulation has been designed to limit the widespread effects that the operations of large companies can have. As new regulations appear these companies either have the resources that enable them to implement the action called for, or they are able to acquire the necessary resources quickly.

Unfortuately the legislation is not restricted to companies in that comfortable position. Although it has been designed with large companies in mind, its application applies to all firms regardless of size. Undoubtedly some of the regulations should apply to all companies, for example those affecting the health of employees and customers. In such cases there should be no exemptions. In other cases, particularly where the cost of conforming would be excessive and unbearable, the requirement to conform should be waived for operations below a certain size; alternatively, if the public interest demands that even small firms should comply, some of the cost of compliance should be borne out of public funds.

## Infant Company Protection

This last suggestion may appear incompatible with previous pleas for a natural and undistorted balance in the size spectrum of commercial and industrial enterprises. The only justification I can see for a departure from the general principle is that it would be in the general public interest. The alternative of leaving small firms to carry unbearable costs would simply destroy many of them. As a result the public would be denied that quite considerable part of the added value that companies create that comes to it through taxation. Over 40 per cent of the total creation of private wealth is for the public use. The payment of a small amount to cover certain costs of compliance with regulations that are in the public interest is an investment with a high rate of return if the firms are kept in business.

My personal experience with local enterprise agencies, assisting in the formation of new small firms, convinces me that the public exchequer should share some of the exceptional risks that they take in their infancy, up to the age of about three years. Like any living creature, the infant company needs all the nourishment it can get to build itself up quickly to the point where it is able to stand on its own feet and cope with the harsh outside world. Few new firms break even before two years; by providing support for a very limited period, the public would be making an investment and in most cases that would produce a substantial flow of tax revenue thereafter. Removal of the requirement to pay local taxes and National Insurance contributions for the first three years would be a small step in the right direction. But more than that is needed if there is to be a reasonably just sharing of the initial high risk. At present the entrepreneur carries the whole of it. Even though more than 40 per cent of all the wealth created by a company from its birth goes to the public, at present the public takes no share of the risks. The new paradigm requires a great deal of innovation, and much of this comes from small firms. It is particularly important in the years to come that people should not be unnecessarily deterred from taking the initial risks. The public should bear its fair share.

## A Call to Action

Can the system ever really be changed to remove the obstacles we have identified and discussed? Can the rules of the business game be so rewritten as to be effective in promoting the New Age of sustainable development?

We should be deceiving ourselves if we did not recognize the strength of vested interest that will oppose these changes. Certainly little will happen unless there is a sufficient body of powerful opinion, particularly among managers and employees, to overwhelm this opposition. The coming decade, during which the new Europe will take shape, will in any case be a period of great change in most European countries. Many of the changes mentioned in this chapter will perhaps be more easily made under the umbrella of the EEC than by each nation in isolation. Even so, a great deal of concerted action will be needed to persuade legislators, and that action will never be taken so long as the deeply felt attitudes and ingrained habits of managers and working people have not first been changed.

## Summary

Although significant movement of the management of business towards sustainable development can be effected under the existing rules of the business game, much more could be achieved under a new set. Nevertheless there should be no delay in *starting* the process of change: the potential environmental and ecological threats are too pressing and it will take a long time to change the rules in the face of strong vested interests in the maintenance of the status quo.

There is certainly no reason why programmes aimed at raising employees' awareness and understanding should not begin immediately a company has decided to move in the new direction: there is no time for delay, because changing habits of thought and action at all levels will not be achieved quickly.

## Notes

* J. Harvey-Jones, *Making it Happen.*
1 Papal encyclical, *Quadragessimo Anno.*
2 S. Brittan in *The Financial Times*, 25 February 1982.

# 10

# New Age Opportunities – Sustainable Technologies

If a man cheats the earth, the earth will cheat the man.

Chinese Proverb

There is more art in saving than in getting.

Benjamin Franklin

It is an ill wind that blows no man profit.

Thomas Fuller

I now want to examine the opportunities for businesses in Europe that a shift to a sustainable development path presents, and to see how different technologies can contribute to the exploitation of those opportunities.

It may seem presumptuous in a book about the management of discontinuous change to attempt to discuss challenges and opportunities. However, what has already been said in earlier chapters about the various elements of the paradigm change provides some useful clues when linked to what is known about technological development. Each company will have to evolve its own solution; but it is useful to know whether a particular change that is contemplated is or is not in the right general direction. I find that most people initially imagine that it must be some kind of retreat from the progress that we have enjoyed and that they fear a deadening contraction as the only outcome. Only when they begin to conceive the unlimited potential of renewable materials and sources of energy do they relax!

## Discriminating Growth for the New Age

Sustainable development does not mean no growth. It offers the most discriminating, efficient and full supply of all the human and environmental needs that are material and energy intensive. It takes the place of the indiscriminate and prodigiously wasteful ways in which we have attempted to satisfy those needs in the past. However, it recognizes that those particular needs, such as food, shelter, clothing, mobility, are limited in quantity, and that excessive consumption is detrimental to the planet and its people. It is important that the quality of goods and services should be as high as possible within the new meaning of quality. But other things like sport, music, art, medical services, education, hobbies, leisure pursuits and religious activities, that require little consumption of energy and materials and that are the source of all that is most enriching in life, can continue to grow without limit.

> In future a great deal more technological thinking power must also be used to give discovery and design a rational direction. We know the tactics of technology; we need to develop the strategy as well.
>
> *The Duke of Edinburgh*[1]

As we considered Maslow's hierarchy of needs (see figure 5.1) we saw that the lower needs (of a physiological kind, of belonging and security) are all limited and can easily be satisfied, whereas our higher needs of self-respect, self-fulfilment and transcendence are unlimited. These higher needs put very little pressure on the earth's resources. On the contrary, they can only be satisfied by human skills and dedication, and by harmonious relationships between people, and between people and the environment. It is the greater satisfaction of *these* needs that is most required in Europe and in other advanced industrial countries. The promise of the age of consumerism, that these higher needs could be satisfied by the unending production of more and more material things, has been a tragic perversion.

## Growth for Developing and Developed Countries

The need for growth in the supply of goods and services to meet physical needs is greatest in the countries of the Third World; but some growth in consumption is also required in industrial countries to satisfy the needs of the inadequately fed, housed and clothed, so that they may enjoy a dignified life. However, the very big reductions in the consumption of materials and energy by the better off majorities (due to greater efficiency and less wastefulness) can more than match the growth in consumption required by the minority, resulting in a huge net reduction in consumption in these countries. There is no doubt that the many things that can contribute to the satisfaction of the full range of human needs are needed across the whole world. That is sustainable development, and it is the business agenda for the future. There are many challenges for all who are involved in industry and commerce. They more than any are in a position to make sustainable development a reality. In 1989 Sir Peter Holmes, wrote 'Concern about our natural environment and our ability to sustain economic development on a global scale are issues of major consequence today. This offers continuing and worthwhile opportunities for industry.'[2]

## Guidelines for Sustainable Development

So we are entering a New Age of changed beliefs and assumptions. Despite all the uncertainty we have to try to see through it and prepare for a different operating environment and market. Forward projections from past trends are not likely to help very much. Nothing is going to change overnight. But this should not make us complacent. The producers of CFCs and banned insecticides are only too well aware of how rapidly revolutionary change can affect a business. As we move into uncharted territory, the greatest need is for some guidelines.

---

**Box 4** *Guidelines for Sustainable Development*

- Maximize personal and business services.
- Do more with less by maximizing maintenance, repair and reconditioning.
- Do more with less by reusing things and recycling materials.
- Do more with less by designing goods for durability and repairability.

- Use processes which minimize pollution and the waste of non-renewable resources.
- Use energy in ways that minimize waste.
- Optimize the efficiency of systems.
- Maximize the sustainable use of renewable energy and materials.
- Design and operate manufacturing and service units on as small a scale as is consistent with the efficient use of resources.
- Use technologies that enhance human skills, are 'user friendly' and match the capabilities of the local population.

These guidelines contrast strongly with those that have influenced past development. For example, for decades we have been producing many goods that were decreasingly durable and repairable: when they were considered to be no longer useful they were thrown away instead of reconditioned. At the same time maintenance and repair have become less important. Non-renewable plastics and synthetic fibres have largely replaced renewable natural materials. Elements of systems have been improved rather than whole systems. Many processes have been polluting and very wasteful of scarce resources. Many manufacturing and service units have grown unnecessarily to a giant size. Much traditional technology has replaced skills and threatened its users. Consequently New Age opportunities are to be found everywhere.

> Everytime you take your supermarket trolley for a spin you are taking part in a referendum about the future of the planet.
>
> *Dr David Bellamy*

## Every Industry must be Reformed

Sustainability calls for an almost total reconstruction of all economic activity. Even the most ancient activities of agriculture and food processing will need to undergo a revolution. Although agriculture is to become more organic – less dependent on fossil fuels and synthetic

> Whoever is generating new technology will conquer the marketplace
> . . . A nation that does not accord the utmost importance to R&D has
> made a decision not to be in business in five to ten years.
>
> *Dr Bruce Merrifield, US Department of Commerce*

chemicals – it will not be simply a reversion to earlier farming
methods. New bioscience and technology will be important contributors
to the new agriculture, providing such things as benign nitrogen
fixation, hybrid plants and improved resistance to disease. In the field
of food processing Unilever sees radical changes in the ways that
wastes will be handled in many areas of the industry. Edible oils
provide a useful illustration of processes which are clean and not
wasteful. A very big change should also take place as commercial food
processing is dispersed to comparatively small, local production units
– for example bakeries, bottling and canning plants and breweries.

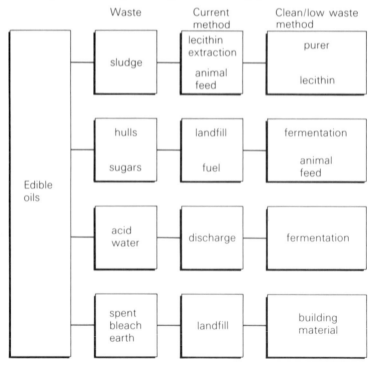

**Figure 10.1** Methods of disposal of waste material from the production of edible
oils. (*Source*: Unilever, 1982).

Building is the next most ancient activity to be transformed, even though it has been much less industrialized than most. Thermal design and durability of construction will be of much greater importance. Materials with high insulating properties will replace the flimsy, heat-conducting types of construction that have been used in the past; and care will be taken to capture and retain as much solar energy as possible, using materials such as Pilkington's Kappafloat glass. Much of the heating will be derived from combined heat and power systems and from heat pumps. We should reject the idea of waste heat from the generation of electricity, and think more about its opposite – the generation of electricity as a by-product of the burning of fuel for heating. Lighting and electrical appliances could use energy more efficiently by drawing power from photocells feeding into storage batteries.

Micro-electronically controlled, precision textile machines should make it possible for the textile and clothing industries to become cottage industries again, using fibres derived from renewable resources rather than from fossil fuels.

The energy supply industries will need to be transformed by using solar, wind, hydro, wave, tidal and geothermal sources much more, combined with the development of systems based on biomass, in which the carbon dioxide generated in combustion is balanced by carbon dioxide absorbed by the biomass during its growth. Coppicing is likely once again to play an important role.

All kinds of transport will be affected. Seagoing vessels should derive part of their power from aerodynamically efficient aerofoils. Road passenger transport poses the most difficult problem largely because we love our cars so much. They have caused death and injury to more people in the last forty years than have all the many wars that took place in the same period. How long we can continue to accept such havoc as the price of our mobility is a question that must surely at some time be seriously addressed. Until that time there are many things that can be done to reduce the carnage. No doubt from time to time and in certain places they will be introduced, but as more people come to own cars across the world, serious road accidents are likely to increase. At some point the free use of cars will have to be stopped. In the mean time Peugeot is already introducing a battery-powered version of its 205 model. There would be a large reduction in the pollution of our city streets if cars were battery-powered. Congestion caused by their widespread use in towns will increasingly attract attention to new forms of passenger road and rail transport. Sheffield's supertrams and the Tribus are early examples. In the air, airships are reappearing; and studies have been made of aircraft fuelled by hydrogen.

Although it is not difficult to imagine the manufacture of foodstuffs, textiles and clothing being dispersed, it may not be thought feasible to do the same with the manufacture of motor cars. However, a motor car is a complicated assembly of many individual parts. Many of these units, sub-units and components are already produced in many different places. They are then brought together in a main plant to be assembled into cars. In recent years low-volume producers of 'kit cars' have begun to appear. At present they mainly supply kits to individual DIY enthusiasts. As the reconditioning of cars becomes more common, it seems possible that the final assembly of high-volume, popular models could be carried out in local workshops that combine the reconditioning of particular models with the final assembly of new versions of the same ones. The skills and equipment required for the reassembly of reconditioned cars are much the same as those needed for the initial assembly of a new car. The same principle could apply to other products that can be reconditioned.

## Every Other Kind of Business Must be Reformed

Whatever the business, sustainable development is going to require an approach radically different from the one pervading the last forty years or so. We can begin to get some idea of the changes and opportunities the New Age presents by testing present practice against the guidelines listed in box 4.

### Personal Services

---

**Box 5** *List of Personal Services*

| | |
|---|---|
| Laundry | Financial advice |
| Ironing | Saving and investment |
| Food and drink preparation at home | Transport |
| | Legal |

| | |
|---|---|
| House and car cleaning | Libraries – books, music, |
| Decorating | videos |
| Clothes making and repair | Museums |
| Gardening | Theatres, cinema, concerts |
| Car and domestic appliance | Sports and fitness centres |
| repair/maintenance | Tourism |
| Building maintenance/repair | Education/distance learning |
| Building improvement | Hobbies – indoor/outdoor |
| Shopping | Arts |
| Home-care of the infirm and | Hotels, camping, caravans |
| elderly | Restaurants, pubs, wine-bars |
| Creches and play groups | Home entertainment |
| Counselling | Spiritual centres |
| Chiropody | Job training/retraining |
| Massage | Medical services |

The unlimited prospects for growth in an age that has to be sparing in the use of non-renewable energy and materials lie in the area of personal services. After decades in which the emphasis has been on material things, personal services are at an early stage of development with great scope for innovation and new initiatives across the wide range of examples shown in box 5. Many of these activities can be broken down into several sub-sections and specialities. Behind many there are also support services that provide the resources for those who finally deliver the services.

The increase in personal services over the last ten years is partly due to the entry of more women into employment. In the home, with limited time for domestic work at their disposal, they like to concentrate on those things they like best. One unpopular domestic chore is ironing. Some enterprising people have identified an opportunity to offer a personal ironing service in the home. Another opportunity has arisen out of the growth of home brewing and wine making. Some people who wish to enjoy the wine get no great satisfaction from the production process and they frequently do not get consistently good results. A house-to-house brewing and wine-making service has been started by one enthusiast. These are two of many examples of comparatively new services arising out of the changes that are taking place. Another important type of service for the New Age concerns the efficient use of energy in our buildings.

## Business and Other Services

Dr Jonathan Gershuny has shown that only about half the people employed in the 1970s in the service sector of the British economy were providing services to ordinary individuals or families.[3] The remainder were serving businesses and various organizations and institutions. The kind of changes in work patterns described in chapter 5 have probably increased the proportion of workers engaged in these services, as major firms reduce their work-forces and call in specialized services to handle work they previously did themselves.

For a long time there has been an extensive list of services available to businesses, many of which have been used by small and medium-sized firms that were unable to justify employing a complete range of specialists full time. These traditional services have been supplemented by a new range arising out of the adoption of information technology. Although this micro-electronic revolution in business has been continuing for more than twenty-five years, it is still in a fairly primitive state. A great deal remains to be done with such things as 'expert systems'. This extension of IT will undoubtedly open up many new opportunities for specialist services.

However, there could be even greater opportunities for growth in a number of traditional business services that have been somewhat neglected, each of which is of critical significance for sustainable development.

## The 4 Rs – Repair, Reconditioning, Reuse and Recycling

The record of industry and commerce in the 4 Rs is somewhat better than that of the domestic sector; nevertheless, far less attention has been paid to it than is required if the best use of scarce resources is to be achieved. Doing more with less demands a major expansion of these labour-intensive, comparatively low-capital activities in all parts of the economy.

In chapter 4 the good economic sense of repair and reconditioning was demonstrated. Extending the useful life of goods by these means is a more efficient and more economically productive use of resources than manufacturing. The opportunities for the development of small and medium-sized businesses that specialize in this area are very great. Furthermore, it is an important area of employment for skilled manual workers.

There is a somewhat limited notion of the recycling of materials. Sustainable development requires its widest use. To illustrate the point, I was involved some years ago in the development of a means of recycling bituminous road materials. Conventional practice required that two inches of road surface should be removed and dumped and that the same amount of new bitumen/aggregate mix should replace it. The new process removed only *one* inch of the old material. A further inch was scarified and treated with a compound. After rolling, a further inch of new material was superimposed. In this way it was possible to repair the road to a standard equal to that of a conventionally repaired surface, with a 50 per cent saving in construction materials and in the energy used in their production.

## Bottles and Cans

It was only in the mid 1970s that the spotlight was turned to recycling in Europe. West Germany was in the forefront with legislation in 1975 that provided a framework for a waste economy programme. Further amending legislation in 1980 gave an even greater emphasis to recycling and the conservation of energy, and the Federation of German Industry has strongly supported the creation of a market for waste materials. Such a market is essential if any progress is to be made. The UK has been slower in taking advantage of the potential; but most other industrial countries have made considerable progress in the last fifteen or twenty years. In the Netherlands, for example, there are bottle bins in shopping and residential streets with the result that 50 per cent of glass bottles are recycled. Several American states have obliged customers to pay a deposit on soft-drink and beer cans. Reverse vending machines then accept used cans in return for money. Oregon took the lead and 90 per cent of cans are now recycled. There is a 95 per cent saving in electricity if cans are produced from recycled aluminium!

## Three Tonnes of Oil from Ten Tonnes of Refuse

When waste material cannot be recycled for its previous application it can frequently be put to a good alternative use. The commonest example is the use of domestic waste as a source of fuel for the generation of steam. But there are more sophisticated techniques. For example, five million vehicle tyres, weighing 50,000 tonnes, are being converted every year in a multi-million pound pyrolysis plant in

> Science discovers 'what is': engineers turn this knowledge into 'things that have never been'.
>
> *Von Karman*

the West Midlands, UK. The products are 20,000 tonnes of light fuel oil, 17,000 tonnes of coke and 7,000 tonnes of scrap steel. Another potentially valuable process is proposed by the Manchester University Institute of Science and Technology (UMIST). It is designed to convert refuse into oil, with ten tonnes of refuse producing three tonnes of oil.

### Take-apart Technologies

For centuries materials research and development has concentrated on ways of creating useful materials from natural resources, and on finding ways of combining different materials, either as alloys or as composites, to produce new materials of different and superior properties. Very little attention has been paid to the reverse process of taking compounded materials apart, or of making waste materials into feedstocks for new production processes. Both of these avenues of development present important commercial opportunities.

## Alternative Materials

A further area of opportunity exists in the use of alternative materials and systems. Substitution of advanced ceramics for some metals is a relatively undeveloped field; and glass fibre technologies and optoelectronics are also ripe for development and application. There are also far less sophisticated alternatives, which may be even more important. The system of wall construction developed by John Parry for use in the Third World could provide, for any country, an inexpensive alternative whose production is based on local soils, consumes little energy and hardly pollutes at all. When a slightly modified example of this system was used for single-storey, experimental buildings in Devon, the amount of energy used for the production of construction materials was about one-seventh of that used for conventional brick construction, and the total cost was about a third.

## Conservation by Separation

Separation processes of gases, liquids and solids will be of great importance in reducing pollution and in making recycling more viable. Membrane systems are more efficient in the use of energy than conventional filters and separators. Here is another area of opportunity in substitution.

## Low-waste, Clean Technologies for the Long Run

There is a temporary need to provide 'bolt-on' devices to clean up dirty plant in order to make it acceptable for the remainder of its useful life. However, 'bolt-on' is not always a satisfactory, long-term solution. Intrinsically clean plants need to be developed wherever possible as successors to the existing plants.

The Bayer Chemical Company, Laporte and BTP Dioxide provide evidence of the introduction of cleaner production processes. For example, they have dealt with the disposal of sulphuric acid waste, from the titanium dioxide sulphate process, by replacing it with a cleaner chloride process. The ICI FM21 membrane cell, which can replace the mercury cell and the asbestos-based diaphragm cell in the production of chlorine and caustic soda, is another example. In addition to its reduced effect on the environment, it consumes less energy. The ECE's 'clean technologies' compendium is recognition that technologies with a low impact on the environment are as desirable as those which are highly efficient in the use of materials and energy.

However, the substitution of an intrinsically clean process for a dirty one may not always be possible. In such cases 'bolt-on' systems to clean up effluent may be a permanent necessity. Examples are to be found in metal industries from which much of the metal contamination of water occurs. Effluent treatment in this industry offers many good opportunities.

## Biotechnologies for a Second Industrial Revolution

Biotechnologies possibly constitute the biggest single cluster of technologies that can contribute to globally sustainable development in the long term. The first Industrial Revolution developed through the interaction of scarce fossil fuels with rocks bearing scarce, inorganic elements. The second will depend increasingly on renewable sources of energy processing renewable resources. Thus biotechnologies can be expected to play an important part both in the creation of entirely new industries and in the replacement of some that are more traditional.

It has been suggested that 'biotechnologies will affect a wide range of activities such as food and animal feed production, provision of chemical feedstocks, alternative energy sources, waste recycling, pollution control, and medical and veterinary care.'[4] The potential can best be shown by the diagram produced by the Celltech Company (see figure 10.2).

Perhaps the most important potential contribution will be renewable energy from biomass. 'Energy crops' can play a very significant part in meeting needs for energy without increasing the levels of carbon dioxide in the atmosphere, provided that a balance is struck between the emissions from combustion and absorption by the biomass. Many opportunities exist, for research and development work, to determine the most suitable crop species for particular local situations, climate, soil condition, rotation periods and end uses. With the necessary scientific information, commercial opportunities will increase as systems that are efficient in the use of energy are brought into operation and fossil fuel 'carbon taxes' are introduced as a means of controlling the greenhouse effect. Options for the use of biomass are illustrated in figure 10.3.

## Training and Retraining for survival

An important impediment to the creation or expansion of many businesses is a shortage of a wide range of skilled people. It is no exaggeration to say that the paradigm change requires that the entire work-force is in need of retraining. This is not only because many new skills are called for, but also because a fresh attitude and outlook are required. Much of the skill training from which small firms traditionally benefited was acquired by people when they were previously employed in large or medium-sized firms. Small firms often lack the necessary resources to provide adequate training. As large companies employ fewer people, and employment in small and medium-sized companies grows, a problem arises as to how and where the necessary training is to be done. Traditionally a fundamental distinction has been made between training and

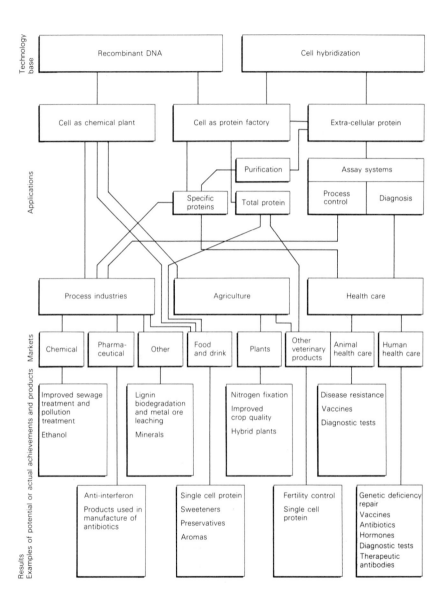

Technology base

Applications

Markets

Results
Examples of potential or actual achievements and products

**Figure 10.2** Some potential applications of biotechnology. (*Source:* Celltech Company.)

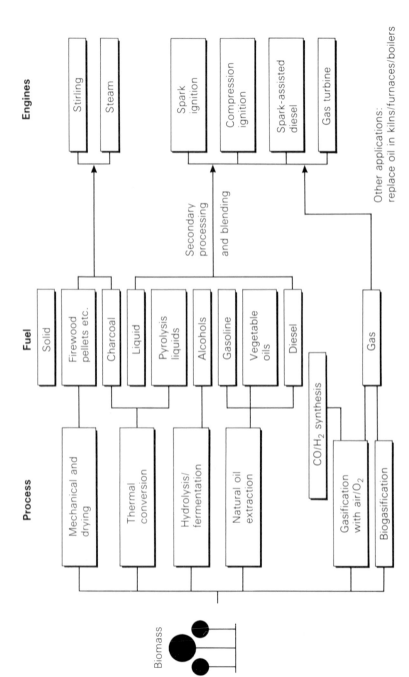

**Figure 10.3** Some biomass options.

education. It may be that, as regards the provision of resources, the fairest solution would be to treat them both as 'personal development'.

## Cooperative Marketing and Purchasing for Profit

Marketing is one of the biggest problems facing small manufacturing companies. If they happen to be supplying a retail market they are often forced to channel their products through wholesalers. As a result a large part of the added value they have created is absorbed by the wholesaler. This is most serious where multiple chains dominate the High Street because, through their purchasing power, they are able to drive very hard bargains with their suppliers. A big opportunity exists in those European countries where marketing cooperatives have not developed as an alternative to wholesaling. They would not only retain the wholesaler's profit for the producer, but would also be able to contribute much more to marketing than mere product distribution. They would tend to be more specialized in the range of products handled, and they would provide a much better feedback from the retailer to the producer. In some businesses they may even undertake product design and development and the purchasing of supplies. Some retailers have been much more receptive than manufacturers to the idea of participation in cooperative purchasing schemes. If small manufacturers are to develop their full potential they will have to overcome their dislike of cooperative arrangements.

The small firm standing alone has great difficulty in competing in a modern market-place in which similar goods are being sold with aggressive advertising and promotion. In several EEC countries ways have been developed in which small firms in the same business cooperate in all aspects of marketing while retaining their independence. Italy has led the way in cooperative marketing with its *consorzi* (consortia of cooperative marketers). Not only have they been very successful in dealing with competition in their domestic markets, but they have also played an important part in establishing small firms' products in export markets. Woollen textile businesses in the Prato area of northern Italy provide an interesting example. Altogether about 46,000 people are employed in some 10,000 tiny firms, and there are another 1,200 firms making and repairing modern, sophisticated textile machinery and equipment. The merchants, *impannatori*, are people expert in the marketing of textiles and they have entrepreneurial flair. They take orders, commission designers, then guide production through a network of small, independent, specialist workshops.

The value of this kind of cooperation has been recognized in the UK. The Cooperative Development Agency (CDA) initiated group marketing projects in 1987. In the first two years sixty groups were formed. Initially the firms seeking to cooperate were consultants, designers and firms with very special skills. Later, groups were formed in the construction industry, and among engineering and telecommunication companies. In addition to providing a comprehensive marketing service on behalf of the group of companies cooperating, CDA can also, if required, provide other common services, such as group purchasing, at low cost. Once the single European market is fully working there can be little doubt that cooperative marketing for small firms is going to play a more important role.

## Franchising – the Bridge between Big and Small

There has been a significant increase in franchising recently. Oil companies have a great deal of experience with their networks of retail service stations, in what approximates to a franchised operation. The companies provide a great deal of expertise for the location, design and equipping of stations and for the range of services that they provide. The selection of dealers, their training and that of their employees are carried out with professional care. Once a station has opened a standard administrative system is provided, and also regular monitoring and support of the dealer's business.

My experience as a marketing executive for an oil company has made me an enthusiast for franchising. One reason for the high rate of failure of small firms of all kinds, and for the poor performance of many others, is the lack of the kind of professional expertise that a modern business needs. Independent franchise operators, with no vested interest as suppliers of a product, can provide the same excellent service that an oil company provides for the operators of service stations.

## Technology Transfer in a Technology Supermarket

A high rate of technological change necessitates fairly frequent changes in both products and processes of maufacture. Although some small and medium-sized firms are very good at developing new products that do not involve changes in technology, many are unable to adapt easily to different circumstances brought about by such changes. Having inadequate resources to carry out costly research and development, they are forced to seek outside sources of new technology. Unfortunately the mechanisms for the transfer of technology to small companies have been few and deficient. In so far as technology could be obtained on licence, it was frequently only available on an exclusive basis that put it beyond the reach of a small firm.

From experience gained in the UK Unit of the Intermediate Technology Development Group, which offered technical assistance to small, British, manufacturing companies, Brian Padgett concluded that a technology supermarket was required to meet their needs, with licences available cheaply and non-exclusively. For the kinds of technology required by small companies, non-exclusivity provides the licenser with the prospect of the best total return, and the licensee with an offer that can be afforded. Technology Exchange Ltd was formed to provide an international supermarket for technology for small firms. The database of offers has built up so that there are, at any one time, about 11,000 items that have been carefully designed so that they may be easily transferred. A system has been developed so that a company shopping for technology can gain cheap access on a pay-as-you-go basis, until a suitable match has been made between the licensee and the licenser. Any business seeking a deal need only specify its manufacturing capability and its markets for it to be put in touch with a range of new opportunities uniquely suited to its particular needs. Its acquisition may have come from any one of 500 sources round the world, some of which are major industrial companies, some individual inventors.

## Independent R&D Laboratories – Sources of Technologies for Small Firms

Independent R&D laboratories are important potential sources for the supply of technologies for small firms. Traditionally they have carried out work on behalf of governments and major and medium-sized companies. Increasingly they market technologies that they have developed from their own resources. As more R&D work is subcontracted by major companies (as mentioned in chapter 7) and as small firms increasingly need frequent injections of new technology, an opportunity is opening up for an expansion of independent R&D organizations.

### Shared 'Managed Workspace' for Small Enterprises

Since the beginning of the Industrial Revolution, industrial and commercial operations have become increasingly concentrated in large urban areas. Movement away from these old centres is under way, and is likely to increase as more and more activity takes place in a dispersed form in small units under the influence of microelectronic technology. The relocation of economic activity presents an important opportunity for the building industry and for commercial and industrial property developers. One significant feature associated with the local enterprise agency/trust movement of recent years has been the provision of multi-occupation accommodation for small firms, incorporating shared basic business services. This has provided an excellent operating environment that was previously denied to small enterprises. A substantial growth in such business accommodation may be expected in years to come.

In the 1980s 'managed workspace' groups have been formed in France, Germany, Switzerland, the Netherlands and the UK. In France, for example, *pépinières d'enterprise* have attracted increasing attention since 1985, when DATAR, the French government's organization for regional economic planning and development formally approved their value in local economic and employment development policy. Managed workspaces are fairly widespread throughout France, with some concentration in the Nord Pas de Calais area, the Île de France and in the Lyon region.

## Summary

In this chapter we have looked at the wide range of commercial opportunities and sustainable technologies that the New Age offers to innovative business people. Each company will need to identify those opportunities that suit it. As Schumacher wrote 'In the excitement over the unfolding of his scientific and technical power modern man has built a system of production that ravishes the earth and mutilates man.'[5] The challenge for this and future generations of business people is to rebuild a society which provides opportunities for everyone to develop his or her potential in ways that are in harmony with the environment, for that is our only means of support. An exploration of possible opportunities and technologies is necessary if that challenge is to be met.

The market opportunities can be easily identified from the guidelines to sustainable development listed in box 4 earlier in this chapter. They involve a marked change in the balance between production and repair, reconditioning, reuse and recycling services, in favour of the latter. Durability and repairability, with energy efficiency where appropriate, will be a renewed focus of quality. Substitution of renewable for scarce non-renewable materials and energy will be another priority. When it is not possible to replace a polluting industrial process with clean alternatives there will be opportunities for 'bolt-on' devices. The adoption of a 'total systems approach' will in many cases reveal new or different requirements for design; and a radically different approach to the design of production equipment, making the best use of human skills, could achieve a better partnership between the human and material elements of business.

As it becomes clear that sustainable development requires a reduction in wasteful freight transport, the ability of cheap micro-electronics to achieve high productivity in short production runs opens up a range of opportunities for the development of small-scale, local production units.

In European and other advanced industrial countries economic growth that is low in material and energy consumption will be largely in personal and business services. Maslow's self-fulfilment and transcendence (see figure 5.1) provide unlimited potential for growth. Past attempts to satisfy these needs with material possessions are being found wanting. The comparatively unexplored approach to their satisfaction through non-material services is an opportunity of high order.

All this adds up to the kind of global development that will not plunder the planet today and leave our children to deal with the consequences tomorrow. As Schumacher remarked shortly before his death, 'It will not be easy to learn economic wisdom. But if we do not the human race may well be numbered amongst the species that have become extinct.'

## Notes

1 HRH The Duke of Edinburgh, *Men Machines and Sacred Cows*.
2 Sir Peter Holmes, Chairman's Bulletin for Shareholders (Shell Transport and Trading), September 1989.
3 J. Gershuny, *After Industrial Society*. Macmillan, 1978.
4 ACARD 'Spinks' Report, London, 1980.
5 E. F. Schumacher, *Small is Beautiful*.

# 11

# Postscript: the World's Search for New Systems

Whilst I have been writing this book news has been coming in week by week of almost unbelievable changes in the countries of Eastern Europe. In Poland, Hungary, East Germany, Czechoslovakia, Bulgaria and Romania there have been popular uprisings; these have led to the downfall of repressive governments that have ruled unopposed for forty years under the patronage of the government of the USSR. The search for a new democratic way within the USSR has been reinforced by the pronouncement of President Gorbachev that there will be no intervention in the countries of the Warsaw Pact that seek political reform. This search is paving the way for the people of Eastern Europe to demand new democratic political and economic systems for their countries.

These popular revolutions are of great significance for global sustainable development, and for many reasons. Although shortages of food and consumer goods have contributed to public dissatisfaction with their centrally controlled economic systems, it is the unquenchable spirit of freedom, the desire for justice and the need to live lives of dignity that have been the main forces inspiring these spontaneous uprisings. Market economies may offer them a promise of greater prosperity, but they are not likely to be impressed by the prospect of replacing monopolistic state control by a form of capitalism that is oligopolistic and in some areas itself tending to become monopolistic. The replacement of dependence on a self-perpetuating state by dependence on self-perpetuating multi-national companies may, seen from a distance, have some small attraction; but it is not the kind of liberty, equality and fraternity that people seek when they are rejecting tyranny. They are going to be searching for another way – a democratic political and economic system with a human face.

## Sustainable Development – a Common Aim for East and West

They approach that choice from the position of their present socialist system. We in the West seek to pursue a sustainable development path, and to do so need to create new domocratic structures and relationships and a new legislative framework in our capitalist system that will enable all people to achieve their potentials. From two entirely different starting points we are both in pursuit of a common end – an economic and political system 'as if people mattered', in which all recognize that the market must play an important part, but not the only part. It will be neither socialism nor capitalism as we have known and experienced them. It will embody a new concept of economics founded on sound humane and ecological principles, beliefs and assumptions such as were outlined in chapter 1.

The environmental crisis is another important aspect of sustainable development that is common to Eastern and Western European countries. Although the former rank lower in the international GNP league table than the members of the EEC, most of them nevertheless have serious environmental problems. Indeed some of the worst pollution and environmental damage is to be found close to Eastern Europe's heavy industry. Many western environmentalists have mistakenly seen capitalism as the sole enemy of the environment. Their gaze cannot have penetrated the Iron Curtain where comparatively little has been done to protect the environment, where efficiency in the use of non-renewable resources lags far behind the unacceptably low levels of the West. John Elkington has reported and explained how the best western companies have responded to increasing pressures for greater care of the environment;[1] and they are now recognizing that environmentally unsound practices are in the end economically unsound too.

Many are also beginning to understand that the environmental crisis opens up new commercial opportunities. As the old barriers between east and west crumble, and western companies become more commercially involved in these democracies, there is a hopeful prospect that their new economies will be developed on environmentally benign technologies. On a visit to the UK, President Gorbachev is reported to have said 'We want decentralization and market forces in industry, and the kind of technical innovation that exists in your ICI.'

The changes in Eastern Europe are also of significance for globally sustainable development because, with some exceptions, their resources of domestic energy and minerals are not such as to encourage them to choose the kind of development that will use large amounts of those resources. Indeed after the experience of recent years they are likely to want to become as self-reliant as possible, building up their production of domestic goods. So sustainable development through the conservation of non-renewable resources will be of great interest to them, as will the construction of an economy that makes the best use of renewable resources. Shortage of capital is another factor that will reinforce this tendency.

## A New Business Philosophy

The question of ownership is obviously going to be a matter of great debate as these countries begin to break away from their highly centralized past. The several models discussed in chapter 7 are likely to be important to them because each places much emphasis on the involvement of workers and on justice. These models go a long way to overcome socialist objections to 'the unacceptable face of capitalism'.

In the year during which the democratization of Eastern Europe began, leaders of the Organization for Economic Co-operation and Development (OECD) countries dramatically acknowledged that the environment now has the highest political priority. For the first time it occupied a prominent place in the Economic Summit of May 1989; and its importance was reinforced at the election of the European Parliament, in June, with the return of an increased number of Green members. The biggest surprise of the whole election was that 15 per cent of the votes cast in the UK were for Green Party candidates.

These were significant political manifestations of an explosion of general public awareness and concern about dangers to health and the environment. No longer were such concerns held only by a small minority of environmentalists. Time after time research into attitudes to specific aspects of health and the environment showed that ordinary people shared the environmentalists' concerns overwhelmingly. The dedicated campaigning work of organizations such as the World Wide Fund for Nature, Friends of the Earth and Greenpeace had at last come to fruition. No longer were they seen by the public as purveyors of eccentric and unjustifiably gloomy ideas.

## A New 'Green' Consumerism

This remarkable change in public opinion made an immediate impact on many companies. In a matter of months a green image was adopted by a wide variety of commercial enterprises. Products began to appear claiming environmental friendliness; and ethical investment opportunities became increasingly popular in the unit trust industry. Although initially the degree of commitment fell far short of what environmental pressure groups were calling for, responsible businessmen and women recognized that there could be no going back. Growing environmental pressures had for years been felt by some to be unwelcome irritants; suddenly they appeared as new opportunities. Dr Otto Koch, a director of the West German chemical company Bayer, stressed that 'the aim of environmental protection consists neither in restoring the past nor in maintaining the status quo, but in creating a contribution to the future. It must be seen as a creative task.'

Due to this positive response from companies pressure groups have gained a great deal of credibility in all parts of society; so the knowledge and expertise they possess can, through cooperation, become creative tools for industries. So long as material consumption continues to increase this does not mean, of course, that the public perception of industry as the prime source of pollution will quickly disappear. Nor does it mean that the task of pressure groups to campaign for reductions in material consumption has changed. These two observations need to be understood and respected by business people.

In the closing years of the 1980s there have been fundamental changes of a different kind both in Eastern and in Western Europe. They have sprung from popular movements reacting against the harm being done to people and the planet; across the continent moral choices have been made. They are choices that have profound implications for businesses. The words of the prophet Isaiah come to mind – 'The people who walked in darkness have seen a great light; those who dwelt in a land of deep darkness, on them has the light shined.'[2]

The initial response of many companies to this new enlightenment has been positive and encouraging. However, there is a danger. It appears that in many quarters environmentally sound economic development is being equated with sustainable development. As I have tried to make clear in chapter 1, sustainable development is much more than that. Although it is true that the imminence of serious environmental problems has concentrated minds wonderfully on the need for immediate action on sustainable development, environmental degradation is not our only concern.

## A New Economics

In the opening paragraph of the preface I mentioned that one of Schumacher's central ideas was the urgent need for a fundamentally different kind of economic development that was sustainable in the widest sense. He had arrived at that conclusion shortly after the Second World War, when he joined the British National Coal Board as Chief Economist. His studies of industrial societies convinced him that we were travelling along a road that must ultimately lead to disaster because we were plundering nature's larder at such speed that it would no longer support us in the foreseeable future. He saw that a form of development that was based on unlimited consumption of fossil fuels and scarce mineral resources was unsustainable. In 1954, at a conference in Germany, he made his first public warning about the long-term danger of economic bankruptcy. He pointed out that for thousands of years mankind had lived off nature's income. Only since the beginning of the Industrial Revolution had we started to live off nature's capital. A fatal flaw in conventional economics was that no proper distinction was made between resource capital and income. They were prophetic words, and there were many more to come in later years; but they fell on deaf ears. At the time the dominating vision in the West was of a technological future that promised prosperity for all. In a wonderful biography of this modern prophet, Barbara Wood, his daughter, writes 'No one was interested in listening to an economist who told them that the future was built on dreams.'[3]

The following year a brief assignment as an economic development adviser to the government of Burma provided him with the experience that was fundamental to his thinking about sustainable development. The different context of Buddhist culture underlined the importance of assumptions and beliefs about society as the foundation of an economic system. There has to be a correspondence between the values embodied in the economic system and the cultural values of the society. The notion that economics has no such values is nonsense. He clearly saw that to superimpose an alien, western economic philosophy on the Burmese Buddhist society would inevitably lead to disaster. The western economic system – whether socialist or capitalist – is based on a scientific, materialistic view of life that is incompatible with the spiritual culture of Buddhist societies. It requires no great imagination to see that the same view of life, which is a historic product of the Enlightenment, is also incompatible with other basically spiritual cultures.

I cannot say with certainty that Fritz Schumacher would have subscribed to all the assumptions and beliefs that I have suggested (in chapter 1) should underpin a sustainable system of economic development. However, I have two reasons for believing that there would be a fair measure of agreement. First, a similar set has been exposed to a mixed group of people who are sympathetic to Schumacher's ideas, and it met with considerable approval. Second, and more important, there is a correspondence between much of the content of this book, which arises out of my own business experience and Schumacher's application of his ideas to practical business matters.

## As if People Mattered

Throughout the book I have emphasized the importance of people, and the crucial role of relationships based on trust and mutual confidence between boards, managers, employees and all other stakeholders. Barbara Wood writes 'As an economist Fritz had one great handicap; he was concerned more about people than efficiency.'[4] He was so for a very good practical reason, and not only because of a genuine interest in their well-being. He knew that only people can create efficiency – or inefficiency. Much of his own personal achievement in the National Coal Board depended upon what he referred to as the middle axiom. New ideas that would not normally have been received with enthusiasm by his colleagues had they been given as instructions were implemented and subsequently welcomed because of his leadership and communication skills. He practised what he preached. Many of these ideas have proved effective and were results of the kind of thinking that I have described in chapter 4. Their effectiveness resulted largely from his unending search to find ways of reconciling freedom with planning and control.

There is a great deal in common between the content of chapters 3 and 5 and two more of Schumacher's favourite themes – the need to keep organizations as small as possible, and the need for all work to be personally fulfilling. As he said, 'We must invest in the reduction of boredom. Stupid work produces stupid or desperate people.'

Corporate ownership was another issue of vital importance to him and it led him to become a trustee of the Scott Bader Commonwealth. His sense of justice and human dignity, and his devotion to the writings of R. H. Tawney, would have put him in complete sympathy with Tawney's plea 'to find some principle of justice upon which human association for the production of wealth can be founded.'

## Technology with a Human Face

He may not have agreed with everything I have written about technology, or with the changes in legislation I believe are required to foster sustainable development. Without doubt he would agree – indeed he insisted – that in the long run a new economic system must be developed on the basis of renewable energy and materials. He believed that technologies should be made to serve the needs of people and enhance human skills, and to be conserving, environmentally benign and non-violent. He certainly recognized that the existing legislative structures have been created to foster consumerism and that alternatives are needed to enable a 'conserver' economy to take its place.

## Democratic Development

However, he would not have looked to governments to lead us away from unsustainable development. He often said that we all have to start building lifeboats. In other words the new economy has to be built *by us all*; then governments will in time respond to our initiatives. His enthusiasm for the work I was doing to promote the development of local enterprise trusts was a reflection of this belief. He warmly welcomed invitations to discuss sustainable development with groups of businessmen and women and trade unionists, because he recognized that Peter Wallenberg, the President of the International Chamber of Commerce, was speaking the truth when he said 'The onus of proving that sustainable development is feasible rests primarily on the private business sector.'[5] He knew that this was going to be difficult. In the epilogue to his book *Small is Beautiful* he makes this very clear. I cannot do better than quote from it.

## A New Economy Grounded in Traditional Wisdom

The 'logic of production' is neither the logic of life nor that of society. It is a small and subservient part of both. The destructive forces unleashed by it cannot be brought under control, unless the 'logic of production' itself is brought under control – so that destructive forces cease to be unleashed. It is of little use trying to suppress terrorism if the production of deadly devices continues to be deemed a legitimate employment of man's creative powers. Nor can the fight against pollution be successful if the patterns of production and consumption continue to be of a scale, a complexity, and a degree of violence which, as is becoming more and more apparent, do not fit into the laws of the universe, to which man is just as much subject as the rest of creation. Equally, the chance of mitigating the rate of resource depletion or of bringing harmony into the relationships between those in possession of wealth and power and those without is non-existent as long as there is no idea anywhere of enough being good and more-than-enough being evil. . . .

We shrink back from the truth if we believe that the destructive forces of the modern world can be 'brought under control' simply by mobilising more resources – of wealth, education and research – to fight pollution, to preserve wildlife, to discover new sources of energy, and to arrive at more effective agreements on peaceful coexistence. Needless to say, wealth, education, research, and many other things are needed for any civilisation, but what is most needed today is a revision of the ends which these means are meant to serve. And this implies above all else the development of a lifestyle which accords to material things their proper, legitimate place, which is secondary and not primary.

The guidance we need for this work cannot be found in science or technology, the value of which utterly depends on the ends they serve; but it can still be found in the traditional wisdom of mankind.

To attempt to make the transition without that conviction would be to follow yet another dream.

There are only two possible routes to global sustainability. One allows successive disasters to force the necessary changes. History suggests that many changes of attitude and behaviour only occur as a result of disaster and the fear that it creates. The alternative, disaster-free transformation demands that businesses bring about a gradual change in the operation of the market, and quickly mobilize the will to accept voluntarily the constraints that sustainable development imposes.

What prospect is there that fiercely competing businesses will be capable of displaying such self-restraint and discipline? Happily there are already encouraging signs in some industries, and I do not doubt these early examples will be followed by others, as understanding grows that nature will not compromise. Companies also understand the value of operating in a free-market economy; and they strongly prefer self-regulation to imposed statutory regulation. In the face of the unyielding demands that global sustainability makes, it is quite likely that business leaders will, whenever possible, pre-empt statutory regulation by accepting voluntary constraints. To resist change until it is imposed by legislation would progressively destroy a free-market economy. Managers must not be blind to that danger.

The constraints need not be burdensome. They need do no more than redefine the framework within which the innovative business game is played. Viewed in this light they can be a positive spur to new adventure. Each company will decide upon its own role and strategy within the new rules of the game. Its vision and its values will be informed by that perception. In pursuit of its objective it will recognize the pre-eminent importance of the human element in the process of adding value. To give expression to that recognition it will seek to create conditions in which all the players are enabled to give of their best, unimpeded by excess bureaucracy. Financial matters will be given their due weight, but they will not be allowed to become a dragchain that holds back innovative progress.

Management of the paradigm change towards sustainable development will be very difficult at all levels. Those who succeed will be those who seek to invent the future themselves, instead of trying frantically to adapt to externally imposed changes; and they are only likely to succeed if they are able to animate *all* the people involved for the common good.

## Notes

1 J. Elkington, *The Green Capitalist*. Gollancz, 1989.
2 *Isaiah*, 9, 2.
3 B. Wood, *Alias Papa*. Jonathan Cape, 1984.
4 Ibid.
5 P. Wallenberg, *Sustainable Development*.

# Appendix:
# The Johnson & Johnson Credo

We believe our first responsibility is to the doctors, nurses and patients, to mothers and all others who use our products and services.

In meeting their needs everything we do must be of high quality.

We must constantly strive to reduce our costs in order to maintain reasonable prices.

Customers orders must be serviced promptly and accurately.

Our suppliers and distributors must have an opportunity to make a fair profit.

We are responsible to our employees, the men and women who work with us throughout the world.

Everyone must be considered as an individual.

We must respect their dignity and recognise their merit.

They must have a sense of security in their jobs.

Compensation must be fair and adequate, and working conditions clean, orderly and safe.

Employees must feel free to make suggestions and complaints.

There must be equal opportunity for employment, development and advancement for those qualified.

We must provide competent management, and their actions must be just and ethical.

We are responsible to the communities in which we live and work, and to the world community as well.

We must be good citizens – support good works and charities and bear our fair share of taxes.

We must encourage civic improvements and better health and education

We must maintain in good order the property we are privileged to use, protecting the environment and natural resources.

Our final responsibility is to our stockholders.
Business must make a sound profit.
We must experiment with new ideas.
Research must be carried on, innovative programs developed and mistakes paid for.
New equipment must be purchased, new facilities provided and new products launched.
Reserves must be created to provide for adverse times.
When we operate according to these principles the stockholders should realize a fair return.

# Index